MICROWINS

DARON K. ROBERTS

MICROWINS

[GO SMALL, BUILD MOMENTUM,
AND TACKLE THE GOALS THAT
ACTUALLY MATTER IN LIFE]

WILEY

Published by John Wiley & Sons, Inc., Hoboken, New Jersey.
Published simultaneously in Canada.

For general information on our other products and services or for technical support, please contact our Customer Care Department within the United States at (800) 762-2974, outside the United States at (317) 572-3993 or fax (317) 572-4002.

Wiley also publishes its books in a variety of electronic formats. Some content that appears in print may not be available in electronic formats. For more information about Wiley products, visit our web site at www.wiley.com.

Library of Congress Cataloging-in-Publication Data Is Available:

ISBN 9781394248162 (Cloth)
ISBN 9781394248179 (ePub)
ISBN 9781394248186 (ePDF)

Cover Design: Wiley
Author Photo: Courtesy of the Author
Graphic design: FaithNiyi

SKY10082108_081924

This book is dedicated to the Donut Council, a collection of six humans that buoys me with love and laughter.

Contents

A Story

Two couples bought property not too far from each other.

One of the men had just turned 30. He and his wife had always dreamed of having a second property. The couple boasted high-paying jobs, had quickly scaled their career ladders, and with extra cash on hand, they decided to buy 20 acres in the mountains. With a newborn on the way, they thought it would be nice to have a place where they could retreat to and get away from the bustle of the big city.

The second man was more than twice the age of the younger man. He and his wife had always dreamed of a place to build their final home. Although they didn't live too far from the mountains, they rarely took the time to enjoy them. Sure, they took a hike here and there, but they spent most of their time at home on their small parcel of land. Having meticulously saved their money for decades, they were finally ready to enjoy the serenity of the mountains they could see out of their window. So, they purchased a plot of 20 acres that bordered the younger couple's property.

On one particular day, the two men encountered each other on the gravel road that led to their new purchases.

One drove a beat up pickup truck and the other drove a shiny new Jeep that he'd rented at the airport. As the two trucks neared each other, the two drivers slowed to a stop.

"Looks like we're neighbors," said the young man to the other as he rolled down his window. "My name is Jim. I just flew in to check out the property. My wife and I live in New York."

"It's a pleasure to meet you, Jim. I'm Franklin, but everybody around here calls me Frank. My wife and I live not too far from here. Just about 30 minutes to the east."

"It's good to meet you as well, neighbor. I'm curious, what are your plans for the place?"

"Well," said Frank, "my wife has had her eyes on this place since we were newlyweds, and we finally saved enough to get it. When I was young like you, I promised her I'd build a cabin for the two of us up here. Gosh, that seems like ages ago. Now, it's time for me to deliver on the promise."

"Well, I know she'll appreciate that. I hope this doesn't come off the wrong way, but you got anybody to help you?"

Frank looked over his glasses. "Do I look like the kind of man who needs help?"

Jim's eyes widened. "I didn't mean it that way. I just meant that it seems like you have a lot of work and could use some help."

The old man chuckled. "Well, as a teenage boy I used to help my uncle build houses in these mountains when all of the city folk decided that one house wasn't good enough for 'em."

As Jim looked away, Frank continued, "We'll just have to see if I can still remember some of what I learned 45 years ago. And how about you?"

"Well, we've always wanted to have somewhere we could go to get out of the city for a while and this part of the country is perfect. I just hired a construction company to break ground so hopefully we'll be able to enjoy the place next summer."

"Sounds like a plan," Frank nodded. "I'm going to come up here every day and do a little bit of work a day at a time."

"How long is that going to take you?" asked Jim.

Frank looked up at the treetops and appeared to be working the math in his head.

"That's a good question, Jim. To tell ya the truth, I don't know. I guess it'll take me as long as it takes me."

"Well," said the young man, "good luck on the build. It was a pleasure to meet you."

"You, too," said Frank. "I guess I'll see you next summer.

■   ■   ■

A year passed. And the two men saw each other again on the gravel road of their first encounter. Just as before, the young man was just coming back from his property and was headed back to the airport.

"Well, look who it is! Howdy, future neighbor. It's been a while," said the old man.

"I just drove by your cabin. It looks great," said Jim. "How in the world did you get that done in such a short period of time by yourself?

Frank chuckled and answered with a question. "I thought you were hiring some builders to put up *your* house?"

"I did, and I can't tell you how many things went wrong. The first builder pulled out at the last minute, and so I had to hire a second contractor. The second contractor couldn't get the materials that he needed, or so he claimed, and so we waited and waited until we finally fired him, too. And now, I'm just hoping we can be done with this thing by next year."

"That's a shame," Frank said. "It's hard to find good help these days."

"You never answered my question," said Jim. "Who helped you build the cabin?"

The old man got out of his pickup truck, walked over to the young man and leaned into his window.

"Well, you decided to outsource your project and I decided to do it on my own. So every day I just did a little here and a little there. I laid the foundation one day. I did a little framing the next. And bit by bit I kept tinkering with the place until I got it done. You were making a house and I was building a home."

Jim looked at the man in disbelief.

"As my daddy would say whenever he'd start smoking a brisket, 'Low and slow, that, my friend, is the only way to go.'"

LOW AND SLOW IS THE ONLY WAY TO GO.

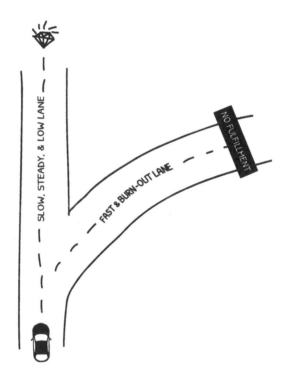

Introduction

The Christmas tree was still standing and my wife was readying our home for a New Year's Eve party the day I was fired. We had been in Cleveland for 304 days. To be exact our home was located on a little plot of suburbia in Berea, a seven-minute drive to the Cleveland Browns practice facility. With three young children at the pre-K level, we didn't choose homes based on school districts, the only criterion that mattered was proximity to the practice facility. Period. As a coach in the National Football League, I spent most of my days (and nights) inside of a dimly lit meeting room tucked away on the second floor watching clips of football plays.

Play.
Rewind.
Play.
Rewind.
Play.
Rewind.
Pause . . . .
Rewind.

I was looking for any tip, the hastened departure a receiver took as he left the huddle, when the ball was coming his way. Or the subtle head nod a quarterback gave before he heaved a deep throw. I would rewatch a single play for one hour, to detect anything (and I mean anything) that could give our defensive players a slight edge. The average margin of victory in the NFL hovers about four points. Four points. That's a field goal and an extra point. Two safeties. It's a razor-thin margin that lies between win and loss.

Let me rewind the story just a bit to give you more context. We had just lost to Mike Tomlin and the Pittsburgh Steelers at Heinz Field in the final game of the regular season. It was December 2013. To be honest, this far removed from that time in my life, I don't remember much about that particular game. I vaguely remember the Steelers being up 14-0 at halftime (I'm sure some of you will Google this; let me know if I am wrong). I remember a few players (and some coaches) looking like they were ready to hit the fast-forward button and get to the offseason. I remember wondering if any of my three kids had slept through their respective naps during the game.

I can tell you what I vividly remember, however, and it is the text message I received just before midnight. Sitting at my computer "breaking down" that day's game, I was readying myself for our postgame meetings the following morning. Fans see games and postgame press conferences. As a coach, you meander through a series of meetings. Pre-practice meetings. Post-practice meetings. All coaches meetings. Defensive coaches meetings. Defensive backs meetings. The gauntlet never ends. Although the season was over, we still had to analyze the game and then begin the long process of grading each player as we went into the offseason. Grading the players would influence who we drafted and signed in free agency. One season was ending but another was just starting.

Or so I thought . . .

The text message simply read: *8 AM staff meeting with the owner*.

Damn it.

I looked at the clock. It was 11:46 p.m. We were 14 minutes away from the start of Black Monday.[1]

My first thought: *We can't be getting fired tomorrow, can we?*

My second thought: *Wait, this is the NFL.*

The entire staff had just arrived in Cleveland. The team's new owner, Jimmy Haslam, had scrapped the coaching staff and front office and handpicked our head coach, Rob Chudzinski. Most of the assistant coaches were on three-year guaranteed contracts. Some of us had four-year deals.

There is a cringe-inducing cliché that you've probably heard before: NFL stands for "Not for Long." Well, it's true. In what may be the shortest termination in the history of firings, owner Jimmy Haslam sat at the end of a long oak table and informed us that he'd fired our head coach, Rob Chudzinski, the previous night.

Damn, he was already fired when I got the text.

That was it. No HR professionals entered the room and checked on our mental health or reassured us that we still had health insurance. Nope, we were done. I remember driving home, walking into the kitchen, and the look on my wife's face screaming, *That's why I never unpack most of the moving boxes!*

Instead she asked, "You okay?" She didn't have to ask what happened. This was my seventh year as a coach. We'd been fired twice. We had frequent hauling miles with U-Haul. From Kansas City to Detroit to Morgantown to Cleveland, we'd crisscrossed the country chasing the next job. More pay. A better title. A bigger office.

"So what do you think is the next stop?"

I shrugged. I was still thinking about what would be the next landing spot. I walked to the refrigerator, yanked a carton of eggs, flipped on the stove, and started scrambling. When I first felt the tug on my hoodie, I ignored it. Then I looked down into the quizzical eyes of my three-year old, Dylan.

He looked at the skillet, he looked at me, he looked back at the skillet.

"You eat breakfast?"

The inflection in his voice was somewhere between the interrogative and declarative. I was unsure whether he was telling me to eat my breakfast or asking me if I ate breakfast. And in one of the lowlights of my fathering career, I ignored the kid and kept scrambling.[2] But Dylan was persistent.

He wobbled into the living room for a few minutes, came back and said, "You ...," pointing a chubby finger in my direction, "you eat breakfast?"

Now, it was clear he was asking a question. I started to answer him, but instead turned to my wife. "Honey, what is he talking about?"

"When was the last time that you had breakfast with Dylan?" I rummaged through my memory bank for the last breakfast I had enjoyed with my son. Not only could I not locate a breakfast, I couldn't remember the last time I had shared a meal with him. The irony jolted me: *I was spending all of my time with other people's sons and my firstborn didn't know that I ate breakfast.*

Meanwhile, my phone was ablaze. Calls and texts were pouring in from around the league.

Just saw the news. Craziness, bro. Keep ya head up.
You good?
Don't sweat it. I got you if you need a landing spot.

I swiped through the text messages. I scoured ESPN for who else was getting fired and predictions on who would land where. But the only thing I could think about was that simple question: You eat breakfast?

What I understand now, that I didn't appreciate in 2013, is that if things aren't going right at home, no quantity of work success can compensate you for the loss. Titles and promotions make for poor traveling companions. Work-life balance is a myth. The scales will never be even. They are in different weight classes. Your work is what you do but your life is who you are.

I had confused my identity with my profession and fractures were showing in the foundation of my home.

That night, I took out a stack of hot pink Post-It notes and wrote one sentence:

Eat donuts w/ DK Saturday.

I went into our bathroom and placed the sticky in the middle of our mirror. Every time I brushed my teeth or washed my hands, those five words stared back at me. I could hear my mind rationalizing my way out of the commitment.

You can do it next week.
Just focus on where you're going to coach next.
He doesn't understand now, but he'll get it when he's older.

Because our head coach had been fired but "technically" the rest of the staff was still under contract, I still had to show up to work every day.[3] So every morning that week, while I brushed my teeth and combed my hair, I stared at those five words.

Saturday finally arrived.

I walked into Dylan's room early that morning.

"You wanna go get some donuts?"

"Donuts?" he asked.

"Yep, donuts. Just you and me. Wanna go?"

"Yes, sir!" he screeched as he ran toward the door.

"Wait! You need shoes, buddy, and your coat."

After straitjacketing him into all of the clothing that a three-year old needs to survive a January outing in Ohio, we pulled into the donut shop, made our order and sat down.

That was a decade ago but what still sticks with me to this day is how the shared meal felt like an out-of-body experience. Even during the "offseason," I rarely had/took the time to sit down with my son in a non-hurried state. It took a job termination for me to recognize how much he needed me, not just to "be around" but to be present.

"Mama, we got donuts!" Dylan yelled as he presented the box of donut holes to my wife.

"That's great honey! I'm sure Daddy will take you again."

The Microwins System

Microwins are small units of victory that chip away at big goals. If you're looking for a complicated system of personal growth, then this is not the right book for you. A stroll through the self-help section of your local bookstore will uncover a pile of manuals, treatises, and how-to books that are much more involved than this system.

My wife and I have five rambunctious children. There are chess meetings. Basketball practices. Reading lessons. Gymnastics meets. On finally getting home after a series of suburban pickups and layovers, I joke with my kids, "Thanks for riding and I hope you'll give me a five-star rating in the app!"

I can't accommodate any system that is more complicated than our pickup/drop-off schedule. Although the microwins system is simple in practice, the work that precedes your adoption of it will require diving into crevices of your mindset that you may feel reluctant to explore.

I get it. This is hard work. It would be much easier to revert back to whatever system you're using now (assuming that you have one). This is the part of the book where I am going to encourage you to *keep going*. I'll encourage you in other places as well (along with providing some insights on *how* to keep going) but for now, I want you to approach this text with an air of openness. Quiet the judgmental voices in your head. Turn your cellphone on "airplane mode" (or completely off). Let's invest the time and energy into our beings that we deserve.

Small ≠ Insignificant

Our world is obsessed with size.

> *How much capital did you raise?*
> *How many followers do you have?*
> *How many likes did you get?*

These numbers make for good happy hour small talk. Your next door neighbor may high-five you in the driveway. But no one is there to celebrate with you when you write your first draft. Or get that first rejection. Or receive the first follow on your account.

These "firsts" are the building blocks of your success story. Yet, to the casual observer they're insignificant and unsexy. That's perfectly fine. Let the world trivialize our microwins.

We are a confetti-driven world attracted to the gathering of crowds. The Microwins System challenges the notion that bigger is better. We embrace and celebrate small units of victory. Why? Because our road to fulfillment and joy runs through checkpoints that don't show up on maps. But it's the small work, the stuff that no one cares to see, that will catapult you to your final destination.

Let me give you an example. When I wrote my first book, my publisher assigned an editor to my project. She tasked me with writing 7,500 words per month. During our first meeting, I listened to her instructions, did some quick math in my head and jotted in my notebook: write 250 words.

I knew that if I allowed my mind to dwell on the 7,500, then I'd probably think my way into writing zero words. But 7,500 words in one month works out to 250 words a day. Could I have set the microwin for 300 words? Sure. Could I crank out 300 words a day? Hell, yeah.

How about 500 words? Absolutely.[4]

What about 1,000 words? Okay, now we're pushing it.

I set my microwin for 250 words and six days a week, from 4:30 to 6:30 a.m., I pulled up to the Strange Brew coffee shop opened up my laptop and typed away. Sometimes it would take me two hours to hit 250, and other times I was done in 20 minutes. Regardless, I stood up, ordered a refill of bad coffee and congratulated myself. Then, I closed my laptop and left.

But, Daron, if you hit your microwin in 20 minutes, why not keep writing?

250 words was the microwin. I choose to reject the notion of "doing more" or "one last rep" or "hustle hard." He who wins a rat race is still a rat. I'm convinced this hustlenista culture is the main driver behind our anxiety-ridden, self-doubting ethos. We judge our growth against the measuring stick of others' progress.

It's past time to shift the focus back to where it belongs, on us.

So today, we are going to cheat. That's right. We're stacking the deck in our favor. We're rigging the game. Instead of zero-one outcomes, we're playing in the gray. No longer will our days be defined by success and failure. We'll rest easier at night knowing that we chipped away at the goals that matter the most, and then we'll wake up and do it again. And again. And again.

When I was coaching in the NFL, I learned the value of committing a laser focus to the smallest details. Those endless nights spent in musty film rooms taught me that monumental things masquerade as menial. This playbook will bring us back to the basics, to the building blocks of success.

The Playbook

As you dive into this playbook, you will uncover and discard the mindsets that hold you back in three phases of life: work, family, and health. This trinity is the command center of our purpose and being. Once that overhaul is complete, you will reconfigure your self-talk to focus on the next small breakthrough. The next small victory. That barely recognizable check mark in the win column that will feed into an avalanche of success.

This book is divided into three sections: *Mindset*, *Mechanics*, and *Momentum*. In *Mindset* we will lay the mental groundwork for implementing the system. In *Mechanics*, we'll dive into the *how* of the system. And in *Momentum*, we'll focus on sustaining positive movement over an extended period of time.

Much of the anxiety we combat on a daily basis is a direct result of being overwhelmed by lofty goals, diminishing time, and compounding responsibilities. This anxiety can give way to burnout and a lack of purpose. I am not here to complicate your life. The goal is to give you a framework that will focus your efforts on the stuff that really counts.

So, have fun with this book. Channel your inner second grader and doodle in the margins. Don't treat it like something you checked out from the library.[5] Mark in it. Scribble. Disagree with me in the margins. Write notes of encouragement to yourself. Star things that inspire you.

And together, let's reimagine what it means to be successful and reclaim the spark we need to live the life we deserve.

YOUR WORK IS WHAT YOU DO BUT YOUR LIFE IS WHO YOU ARE.

Mindset

From my experience coaching athletes and executives, I found that most people prefer to fast-forward straight to the strategy. "Just give me the answer" is a common refrain of people who miss where the real work begins— the mind. In this *Mindset* section, we build a mental framework that will support our persistence and growth in the Microwins System.

Here is a brief summary of the chapters in this part:

Chapter 1: Principle 1: Embrace Your Coffin

Does knowing that you will die affect how you choose to live? Well, it should. With Principle 1, we start the microwins journey by confronting mortality.

Chapter 2: Principle 2: Time Is Made, Not Found

The days are long but the years are short. In Principle 2, we unearth the natural resource that everyone claims is in short supply.

Chapter 3: Principle 3: Wage War Against Your Status Quo

It is time to take up arms. This war to control the narrative of your life is a daily slugfest featuring you versus you. In Principle 3, we train and sharpen our weapons for the fight.

Chapter 4: Principle 4: Wiretap Your Mental Chatter

Did you hear that? The voices in our head are not an aberration. In fact, some of them are real enough to cause permanent damage to our psyches. In this chapter we learn how to tap in and tune out the self-destructive stories that we tell ourselves and engineer a new soundtrack to our story.

Chapter 5: Principle 5: Go Small to Get Home

This final principle primes us for life in the slow and steady lane.

1

Principle 1: Embrace Your Coffin

We are going to die.

This is the opening line to every keynote that I deliver, whether I'm standing in front of a crowd of investment bankers or schoolteachers. And every single time that I utter these words, there is an audible gasp in the room. I can feel the event organizer squirming in the back of the room with a look on her face that says, "Should I have hired this guy?" People turn to look at each other. Some of them mouth to their neighbors, "Did he just say that?"—to which I respond from the stage, "Damn right, I said it!"

When I was growing up in East Texas, I'd hear people ask my grandmother about her plans. Whether she hoped to go to the store, church, or bank, the coda to her itinerary was always the same: "That is . . . ," she'd say, "if the Lord says the same and the creek don't rise."[1] In short, she was saying this: "Here is my itinerary, but let's see what the universe has to say about that." She recognized that what *she wanted* and what *would happen* were two distinct realities.

Our first principle, Embrace Your Coffin, challenges us to acknowledge and honor our temporary status on this twisting sphere we call earth. Scientists estimate our planet has been in existence for 4.5 billion years, give or take a couple of million. The average American lifespan is 77.5 years. I know it's been a while since many of you were in grade school, so I'm going to put the average lifespan in the numerator, the earth's age in the denominator and the number we get is $1.72222222e^{-8}$. Can't remember the rules of exponential numbers? Don't worry, me either. Here's the key takeaway from the math: the amount of time we are alive compared to the life of the earth is small. Tiny. Miniscule. Negligible.

But, that is not to say that our existence is insignificant. Our words and actions sow ideas into the people around us. Those beneficiaries, in turn, sow seeds into the people around them and the cycle continues. This spillover effect is potent enough to alter the future of people we'll never know. And it's this fact alone that should inject a level of intentionality into our existence. We should approach life with a gentle sense of urgency.

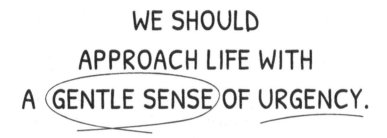

WE SHOULD
APPROACH LIFE WITH
A GENTLE SENSE OF URGENCY.

Gentle Urgency

For eight years, I taught undergraduates at the University of Texas at Austin. Over the course of that time, I had 2,842 students. As I sat down to craft my first syllabus, I thought, *What are the things that I wished I had learned about as an undergrad?* The list was long: vulnerability, empathy, and budgeting to name a few. As I worked through the texts for the course, meticulously charting the blueprint for "Gameplan for Winning at Life," one thought kept nagging me.

What about mortality? To be sure, I encountered mortality in college. I was a Plan II major with a minor in classics.[2] Philosophy, history, literature, genetics, sociology. These classes featured various ways of looking at mortality. But what about meaning? What could I, as a college professor, do to incite my students to think more deeply about their place in the world and the meaning of their lives?

The first couple of years, I sidestepped the question until my mentor texted me with an unusual command:

Read David Brooks's NYT article. It's in today's paper.

My mentor has a penchant for cryptic texts, but when he types, I listen. And so I pulled up the article, "The Moral Bucket List." Brooks writes: "It occurred to me that there were two sets of virtues, the résumé virtues and the eulogy virtues. The résumé virtues are the skills you bring to the marketplace. The eulogy virtues are the ones that are talked about at your funeral—whether you were kind, brave, honest or faithful."

I took a deep breath. This Brooks guy was getting personal.

I learned a tough lesson during the first seven years of my professional life: Job titles make for poor traveling companions. At first, I thought the sexy brands that I had worked for—United States Senate, Kansas City Chiefs, Detroit Lions—would satisfy me. In the short term, they armed me with a sexy introduction. We have all been to the happy hour that masquerades as one big comparison party.

TITLES AND PROMOTIONS
MAKE FOR POOR
TRAVELING COMPANIONS

The inevitable, "It's so nice to meet you! So what do you do?" is code for, "Let me figure out if you're worth talking to." My life had revolved around trying to impress people who weren't even impressed with themselves. And so that night, I decided to write my eulogy.

What did I really want someone to say about me?

I imagined myself lying in a pine box. I even toyed around with the idea of asking a local mortuary to let me spend the night in a coffin as an experiment. No tweets. No business cards. No email. Just Daron lying in a box.[3]

What was interesting to me about what I wrote was what it did *not* contain. I didn't list the sexy stuff that we throw on our LinkedIn pages. Degrees and awards seemed inconsequential. Who would give a damn that I went to Harvard Law School? And who would care that I was the Big East Recruiter of the Year? No one, at least no one who mattered to me.

But what did matter, however, was how I made people feel during my time on the earth. That was the nagging question that kept percolating to the surface. Not *what* but *how*. Would any of my lessons land with my children? Would they remember me being present in their lives? Not merely around but *present*? Would my wife feel I had loved her? Not the love of perfunctory farewells, but real love—the sterner variety.

This was April 2015 so I still had plenty of time to embed a eulogy writing exercise into my syllabus for the fall. I intentionally placed it at the end of the semester, tucked far below the midterm so as not to alert anyone, except for my teaching assistants.

I remember that fall semester as being one of my largest classes, numbering close to 300 students. As expected, no one uttered a word about the assignment until after Thanksgiving.

Professor Roberts, you want me to write my eulogy?

Yes.

But, that means that I'm dead.

Theoretically, yes.

Are you being serious?

Yes.

One of my teaching assistants asked for a meeting with me.

"Professor Roberts, you know that I respect you, but during section today, a few students made some convincing arguments for not writing the eulogy and they asked for an alternative assignment," she said.

Dive into Darkness

In class the next day, I led the class in a moment of breathing. You could feel the tension rise into the rafters. I thought of how this challenging assignment coincided with the final exams they were taking in their other classes. With holidays and travel around the corner, these young people were anxious, stressed, and scared.

The brain wants to protect us. Its job is to keep this vehicle we call our bodies humming along at the speed of homeostasis. Our brains—a three-pound ball of proteins, fat, water, carbohydrates, and salt—is built however for survival, not thrival.[4] Our goals (the big, hairy, scary ones that keep us up at night) lie just north of the homeostasis line. Just thinking about those goals is enough to increase our heart rate and trigger the release valve on our cortisol tanks. I like to think of a cortisol release in the body like an indoor fire sprinkler. Once the smoke from that overcooked chicken reaches the alarm, water rains down. It's a protective device, but it can also be an inhibitor for action.

As I listened to the purr of my students' exhales, I began to empathize with their fear. Turning back to the assignment, I encouraged the undergrads to reimagine the exercise as a celebration. I compared the challenge to a deep-sea expedition. The floor holds both wreckage and treasure, but you can't get to the latter until you wade through the former.

Well, they did it. I expected some form of mutiny or even worse, a pile of half-hearted eulogies, but I wasn't prepared for the sincerity. Sitting on my couch with a stack of papers in my lap, I read every eulogy over a two-day period. If I'm honest, the experience felt like a never-ending funeral. Not only did these undergrads complete the assignment, but each one of them dug deep. They painted intricate landscapes of *who* they would become and *how* they would improve the human condition. I left the University of Texas a couple of years ago, but to this day, those eulogies are my most prized possessions. I've lost the plaques and medallions that I received for teaching awards. But in the northwest corner of my garage stands a stack of banker's boxes that contains every eulogy that was written. Here are a few excerpts:

> *From her days working for Teach for America, students of Catherine remember how enthusiastically she taught math. Every day was a surprise and she exhibited the patience they needed to learn the algebra they hated.*
> *Without Gerald's encouragement, the author Drake Simpson says he wouldn't have written his first book.*

She leaves behind a host of nieces and nephews. Their fondest memories are of her infamous "Samantha Summer Camp" sessions hosted at her cabin in Maine each year.[5]

Notice the feat that these undergraduates pulled off. First, they confronted the fear of thinking about their death. Then, they embraced vulnerability and used their imagination to create a picture of their future selves. For many of them, it was the most challenging assignment they'd completed in school. But they pushed through the agitation.

Confronting our mortality exercises our sense of urgency. It reframes failures from catastrophic to instructive. When we confront death with a vulnerability, it frees us to reimagine how we can leverage the time we have today.

In an interview, Maya Angelou was asked, "You're not afraid of life?" to which Angelou responded, "No." The interviewer couldn't seem to understand her answer, so Angelou continued: "I gave in to [death] which was a great, freeing production for me. Once I really admitted that I would die. That it is the one promise I can be sure will not be reneged upon. Once I understood that, then I could be present. And I'm totally present all the time. I try now, I don't make it all the time, but I try to bring all my stuff here in this studio. Everything I've got is here. And when I leave here, everything I got will be in that taxi."[6]

To close this chapter, let's take a deep dive.

Deep Dive: My Eulogy

First, take a deep breath. I understand this work may be more unsettling for some of you than others. So take as much time as you need to close your eyes, quiet your body, and breathe with intention.

Let's craft *your* eulogy. Don't try to get Shakespearean with it. No one is grading what you write. Make this exercise personal, and this is not the time to be modest. Let's build an aspirational blueprint for the rest of our lives.

Imagine that you are your best friend, and you're standing before an assembly of people who are attending your funeral. What mark do you want to leave on the people around you? How would you want to be remembered?

_____

_____

_____

_____

_____

_____

_____

_____

_____

_____

_____

_____

_____

_____

_____

_____

_____

_____

_____

_____

_____

_____

_____

_____

_____

_____

_____

_____

_____

2

Principle 2: Time Is Made, Not Found

Merriam-Webster defines *busyness* as the state of having or being involved in many activities.[1] Seems fairly benign, right? Well, let's put busyness in perspective.

How the Busyness Keeps Us from the Business

Life is a short trip. We have to be maniacal about the way that we spend our minutes. While at Starbucks the other morning, I overheard two friends bumping into each other:

Busy Person: Hey, it's been too long. How have you been?

Busy Person 2:   *Swamped. We just picked up another account and Jim's out of the office on PTO, so it's all on me. I'm up to my ears in work. And for some reason, I decided to get one of the upstairs bathrooms renovated.*

Busy Person 1:   *Stop it! Same on my end and I'm leading up the gala this year, so we're already looking at venues and of course Madison decided to do travel volleyball this year so we're in a different city every weekend, and I just got assigned to this new client who is a complete mess and emails me on weekends and . . .*

This pickleball match of busyness might be still going on had it not been for an overzealous barista yelling, "Jessica!"[2]

When I entered the professional world, I was naive. I was easily impressed by people's busyness soliloquies. I would always walk away from one of these jousting matches with a feeling that I wasn't doing enough. I'd wonder, "Should I be doing more? Am I doing enough?"

Can you relate? We live in a world where Instagram, TikTok, LinkedIn, and every other social media platform broadcasts the goings and comings of people in our circle. Our phones are portals into the "private" lives of public people.

I Don't Have Time

Intention without execution is dead. When we say, "I don't have time" what are we really saying? We've all heard the nails-on-chalkboard cliche, "We all get the same 24 hours."

That's rubbish. Sure, the sun rises and falls and the clock ticks and tocks but this gift we call time is not universal. And it's not some fungible sum of seconds or minutes.

INTENTION WITHOUT
EXECUTION IS DEAD.

Some of us have kids, some of us don't.
Some of us work from home, some don't.
Some of us have dogs, some don't.

As the father of five incredible little humans, I understand that adulting can be best described as a form of high-intensity interval training and on any given day, our body's check engine light could rear its neon orange head.[3] Each of us stands at the center of a universe crafted by responsibilities. But inside of that universe lies choice. We make decisions about who and what gets our attention. So within that seemingly benign statement *I don't have time* is the **Invisible It**.

The Invisible It

Remember back in grade school when we learned about the invisible you? I can remember Mrs. Campbell saying something like *A command still has a subject. It's the invisible you.* I remember looking at her and thinking, *An invisible you? Like the Casper of the English language? I don't buy it.* But, I did what American schoolchildren do, nodded my head and starred the point for a future quiz.

What is the Invisible It? Well, embedded at the end of *I don't have time* is "for _____." Think of the Invisible It as the object or activity that you're rejecting when you say *I don't have time.*

> *I don't have time* <u>for you</u>.
> *I don't have time* <u>for writing</u>.
> *I don't have time* <u>for reading</u>.
> *I don't have time* <u>for gardening</u>.

The mindset that will empower us to reclaim our lives begins with owning the rejection we so easily dole out to the things we care about most. Every time we choose one thing, we reject all other things. Choosing to Netflix for three hours or scroll through the feed or answer that client's email at 2:07 a.m. is a choice. And we are the sum of our choices.

My Name Is _____ and I'm a Yesaholic

In a previous life, I was a card-carrying yesaholic. I would be invited to meetings, happy hours, strategic planning sessions, meetups, dinners, nonprofit boards, galas. My default response was to say yes to everything.

This philosophy changed in June 2017. I was sitting in a valet line, preparing to enter my second banquet of the weekend. And before I knew it, I just started crying. Let me rephrase that, I was full-body weeping, the kind of crying that sends your body into convulsions. The mere thought of sinking my teeth into one more subpar crème brûlée. Answering one more, "So what do you do?" question. Clapping for one more coma-inducing speech. Just thinking of the inevitable turn of events that would greet me inside of that ballroom at the JW Marriott was enough to turn my stomach.

"Welcome to the JW, may I have your cell number?" the valet attendant asked.

I looked at him, put the car into "drive" and pulled away. I couldn't do it. I was suffering a slow death by a thousand dinners.

■　■　■

"Wow, that has to be the record for the shortest banquet in the history of banquets," my wife quipped as I walked through the front door.

"I couldn't do it," I said, throwing my keys on the living room table.

"Caught a whiff of the chicken?" she chuckled.

"I didn't even make it into the hotel. I drove straight through valet."

"What?"

"Yep, just kept going."

"Well, good for you. You shouldn't have said 'yes' in the first place."

And she was right. I wasn't even supposed to be at this banquet, but one of my friend's law firms bought a table, and my buddy needed to fill some seats. A text the day before simply read: *Hey, man, you want to help me fill this table up tomorrow?*

As I texted my buddy that I wasn't going to be able to make it, I sat nervously waiting for a response.

Five minutes. Nothing.

Thirty minutes. Nothing.

Finally, an hour later he responded: *All good! You're not missing ANYTHING.*

I let out a deep sigh of relief. But, then I wondered why I even needed that message to feel comfortable with my decision to not show up. And more important, why did I always say yes?

Why We Default to Yes

So, why don't we say no more often? Here are a few theories:

1. We don't want to let other people down. "If I tell her no, she'll be disappointed."

2. We want to keep our options open. "If I do this thing that I don't want to do, then it may lead to a thing that I will want to do."

3. Both A and B.

Raise your hand if you enjoy letting people down?[4] That's what I thought. For as sinister as the world can seem sometimes, I do believe there's a kernel of goodness in all of us. And that goodness means that on some emotional level, we care about the feelings of others.

But, let me ask you a question: "How would you feel if *you let you down?*"

Think about it. You arrive at this world with one you. No one is going to make any more versions of you. You're a one of one. And as we discussed in Chapter 1, time is a precious gem, one that deserves to be protected.

What if we inserted some strategic selfishness into our decision-making apparatus? I know the word *selfish* will conjure all varieties of demons and ghosts. Keep them at bay and hear me out.

Our brains are situational inflators. It tends to expand the perceived repercussions of any single act. How many times have we believed that our life was over, or that we would never recover from getting laid off, or that we would never find love again. This tendency to envision the worst-case scenario comes into play as we're deciding whether or to accept or decline an invitation. As someone who has been a card-carrying decliner since 2019, I'm going to let you in on a little secret: most people don't care.

I know. It's shocking. They don't care. They don't care that you didn't go to the reception or turned down the brunch. And the people who do care enough to hold a grudge are not your people. The people who care about you, not in some transactional-keeping-score-by-the-day kind of way, understand that your no isn't a personal attack on them. They'll understand that you need space to thrive.

The right people will get it. The people who care about your mental welfare and need for space will understand. And the ones who don't, won't.

Expanding the Surface Area of Opportunity

The second theory is a refrain that I hear quite a bit. I coached corporate executives for seven years before winding down my practice, and what would begin as a desire for help with time management always ended with training my clients in the ways of saying no. Coupled with their inability to say no came a fear of missing out. Here's the rub: the logjam of yeses left no room for them to say yes to the real work they needed to do. A calendar filled with transactional commitments leaves no room for the transformational.

You Are What You Cannot Say No To

Let's play a game. Think of the last time you committed to something you didn't want to do. Remember that ache in your gut when you read the email? That feeling was your future self-screaming, "Don't do this to me! Please, Daron, don't make me go to that committee meeting!"

A gradual collection of yeses over time snowballs into one big no. I liken this experience to grocery shopping. My wife discourages me from visiting our local grocery store. Why? Well, I walk into the store with a list of items and invariably leave with three times the number of things on my list. In many ways, this mirrors our approach to opportunities. We spend our time collecting yeses.

Yes to the board seat.
Yes to the nonprofit.
Yes to the task force.

So, when we get the rare chance to say yes to something we actually want, we don't have the space to make room for it. Here's a quick story from my life to illustrate the point.[5]

When I was working at the University of Texas, someone asked me to serve on a task force. Let's call her Debbie. I view task forces the same way I view company retreats. Nothing wastes more time and money than a task force or a company retreat. They both fall into the purgatory of let's-sit-around-the-campfire-and-commit-to-doing-s#*!-we're-never-going-to-do.

Anyway, I agreed to join.

I know you're a badass and all, but there is always somebody else who can replace you. It's painful but true. Oftentimes, when people say something like, "But we really need your input on this panel! You will bring such a unique perspective to the conversation," what they're really saying is, "I really don't want to ask someone else, so please just say yes so I can get on with my day."

Back to my story.

So, after the third task force Zoom, I attempted to stab my eye with a V5 Precise pen. Just looking at the calendar entry would make my stomach churn. I had homework for this damn thing. I had to submit written work. I felt like a hapless grad student again.

Life has a twisted sense of comedy. While writing part of the committee's report, an email plopped into my inbox. An online magazine asked me to write an article on my favorite topic: writing. The turnaround time was 48 hours.

"Do you think you could swing it, Daron?"

Here's a paraphrase of my answer: "I really wish I could, but unfortunately I don't have the time." As I typed each word of that email, I became more and more angry. I cursed the task force. I cursed the university. And finally, I unloaded the blame at the only guilty party: me. It wasn't Debbie's fault that I said yes. She didn't hide the ball on the time commitments or my obligations. She was transparent. There would be both scheduled and ad hoc meetings. We would also be required to craft write-ups within our subcommittees. With this knowledge and my experience in the bureaucratic sinkhole also known as higher ed, I willingly said yes.

I was the guilty party.

Let's think of a yes as an option. In finance, an option gives the buyer the right to buy or sell an asset at an agreed-on price on a certain date. When we say yes, the purchaser of that yes acquires ownership in our most valuable asset: time. In the investment world, dealing in options is a dangerous game. One makes assumptions about what will happen in the future. If the market agrees with the prediction, all is well. If the market acts in a way that we don't account for (which it has been known to do), you're on the hook.

And what complicates matters even further is the planning fallacy. In 1979, psychologists Daniel Kahneman and Amos Tversky confirmed what we've known for millennia. Tasks always take longer than what we predict. Always. Our minds tend to gravitate to frictionless visions. We fail to account for the inevitable loss of motivation and exigent life circumstances.

The Two Times Principle

I do not trust me. Let me put that a different way, I don't trust my predictive abilities. So when I attach a unit of time to a future project (sitting on a task force or writing a book), I always double my estimate. For example, when I started writing my first book, *Call an Audible*, I banged out what I thought was a flawless 10-page introduction in three hours. When I got home that evening, I told my wife, "This book will be done in three months!"

Well, it took me two weeks to realize that I was dead wrong. Some days I felt like writing, some days I didn't. Some days the words flowed easily. Some days they didn't. Some days my keyboard felt like a warm pillow, and at other times I wanted to throw my computer through the window of the Strange Brew coffee shop.

And what do you know? Three months turned into six months.

So, regardless of how convicted I am about a time estimate, I always double it. Why is this important? Well, as we're reclaiming ownership of our time, we have to embrace the reality that deep work takes time. It's not a Hot Pocket. And with this understanding that it will take time, we must reserve and guard large parcels of time to cultivate the work we care about the most.

Our professions.

Our families.

Our bodies.

The work in these domains of our life will require more seconds, more minutes, more hours than we can estimate.

Mind the GAP

A few years ago, my wife pulled me to the dinner table for an intervention. I had a problem. Every time someone asked me to donate to their cause, I would.

Will you support the building of water wells in Uruguay?

Sure!

Hey, Daron, can you donate to this camp that helps foster kids learn a second language?

Hell, yeah!

Hey, Daron, will you support Champions for Canines?

Hell, yeah, I will! How much do you need?[6]

With each fulfilled request, Hilary watched our philanthropic numbers shoot through the roof. Something had to give. We decided to create a personal giving policy. We drew a border around two nonprofits and agreed that 100% of our annual giving would go to those two groups. Now came the hard part: saying no in a consistent and kind way.

So, we came up with the GAP method. GAP stands for: gratitude, acknowledgment, and policy. It simply works like this:

Gratitude. Thank the requester.

Acknowledge. Recognize the organization.

Policy. Share your policy.

Let's walk through a real-life example. While writing this book, a local nonprofit asked if I would donate to their cause on Giving Tuesday.[7] The nonprofit does great work, but so do all of the nonprofits that reach out to me for donations. Here was my response:

> Hey, Sarah! Hope you're doing well! I love the mission and impact of _____.
> My wife and I have two nonprofits that receive 100% of our annual charitable giving, so although we won't donate to your cause this year, we thank you for thinking of us!
> Sincerely,
> Daron & Hilary

That's it: 47 words.

In fact, here's the template that is saved as a draft in my Gmail:

> Hey, _____! Hope you're doing well! I love the mission and impact of _____. My wife and I have two nonprofits that receive 100% of our annual charitable giving, so although we won't donate to your cause this year, we thank you for thinking of us!

For other requests, unpaid board seats, steering committees, and so on, I use the GAC method.[8]

Gratitude. Thank the requester.

Acknowledge. Recognize their work.

Craft. Share your work.

Here's an example, courtesy of Gmail:

> Dear Jimmy,
>   Thank you for thinking of me for this opportunity to serve as a board member. _____ does an incredible job of catapulting at-risk youth in our community.
>   At the moment, I am focusing my efforts on completing a manuscript, so although I won't accept the nomination, I wish both you and the organization much success.
> Sincerely,
> DKR

Here's what I've found: most people will respect your decision. I've received hundreds of replies from people who wrote:

> *Completely understand! Let me know when the book comes out!*
> *Sounds so exciting! We will keep you in mind for future opportunities.*
> *I love your discipline; I wish I could do that!*

Not once has someone responded with *You're so selfish*. And in fact, *if* someone did respond that way, then I would view the episode as the universe nudging me to serve an eviction notice to the relationship. We all have people in our lives who we think are invested in us, when in reality, they are invested in what we can provide to them. Never confuse the people in your circle with the ones in your corner.

Your circle is a wide net. There are LinkedIn connections you've never met and high school classmates you will never see again. The barriers to entry are low for a circle. Any connection will do.

But your corner, this is another realm. Members of this select group get emergency calls. They're the ones who tell you the truth. They'll be the ones who show up at your funeral. And the people in your corner will understand when you need to take and make time for you.

Deep Dive: GAP Practice

You just received an email from someone asking you to join a planning committee. (I know that even role-playing this scenario can be traumatic, so if you need to put this book down and take a brief walk, feel free to do so.)

Let's practice the GAP. Craft your email response below:[9]

_____

_____

_____

_____

_____

_____

_____

_____

_____

_____

_____

_____

3

Principle 3: Wage War Against Your Status Quo

D eath will visit us all. It comes quicker to those who revel in an unchallenged life. Our existence is too short for an early surrender to the status quo.

I Declare War

The month of January is what I call *tune-up time*. During the first four weeks of the year, I subject myself to a battery of physical tests to gauge how my body is holding up. My primary physician, let's call him Dr. Fitzgerald, is one of those doctors who is both knowledgeable and funny. On a cold morning this January, I sat in his office. My mind was thinking of how much I wasn't looking forward to that oversized popsicle stick going down my throat.

Dr. Fitzgerald: *How have you been, Daron? It's been a year. Is the family doing well?*

Me: *Been doing well. Chasing kids, evading the IRS, you know, the usual.*

Dr. Fitzgerald: *And how does it feel to be 45? Happy belated birthday.*

Me: *Feels okay. I guess this is the halfway point, huh? I'm pushing through this midlife crisis.*

Dr. Fitzgerald: *Midlife? Let's hope you're right. The actuaries would say you've probably already crossed the midpoint.*

Me: (Silence)

Inner Me: *Damn.*

Dr. Fitzgerald: *Let's keep exercising and eating right and we'll beat the projections. Deal?*

Me: *Deal.*

On the drive home, I thought about his words. *You probably already passed the midpoint.* The thought was sobering. Although his words stung a little, I had to admit, the doctor was absolutely right. I had lulled myself into believing that

I had reached some mythical midpoint when I hit age 45, but the science disagreed. The actuarial charts say that making it to 90 would be quite the feat for me given my demographics.

I'm sure you picked up on this point, but did you notice how I missed my actual midlife crisis? I was six years late to the party. The episode illustrates just how powerful the human brain is. *We are who we think we are.*

Let me give you an example. My next door neighbor is probably in his late 70s, but he doesn't look it. Every morning, whether it's January or July, he's bopping out of his front door in some Skechers and heading for his walk/run. He's the kind of guy who does that animated style of speed-walking, arms pumping and hips twisting.

Anyway, one day I yell to him from the driveway, "Looking good, young man."

Turning to look at me he said, "Damn right, I'm young and look good. Who's got it better than me?"[1] I watched my neighbor trot down the road with a smile. Somewhere in his life, he'd made a decision that he was going to call the shots. He was going to powerwalk all over the actuarial charts.

I want you to commit to something right now: *I declare war on my status quo.*

Did you say it? Let's try this again and this time, say it with your chest: *I declare war on my status quo.*

I DECLARE **WAR** ON MY
STATUS QUO!

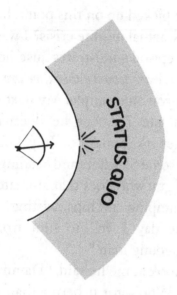

Who Were You Going to Be?

Let me ask you something. Who were you going to be before the experts got involved?

WHO WERE YOU
<u>GOING TO BE</u>
BEFORE THE EXPERTS
GOT INVOLVED?

Take a mental jog back to when you were a kid. If you were anything like me, you were strung out on starbursts and pop tarts. Television shows were portals to a land of possibilities. Every show enticed me to choose a new adventure.

I watched *Doogie Howser, M.D.*, and said, "I want to be a doctor."

I watched MC Hammer glide across the screen and yelled, "I'm gonna be a rapper."

I watched Ken Griffey Jr. effortlessly yank baseballs into orbit and I'd say, "That's me! I'm gonna be a pro baseball player."

Never mind that I: (1) hated science, (2) had mediocre rhythm, and (3) boasted a .206 batting average in Little League.

The beautiful delusion of youth imbues each one of us with a belief that we can be or do what we see. Last weekend, I eavesdropped on my children during one of their role-playing sessions. Here's my best transcript of their conversation:

Delaney: *Okay, on this trip, I'll be the astronaut and you'll be the space police officer. See if you can catch my rocket!*

Sydney: *Got it. I'll make that car alarm noise when I'm close so you know when to take off.*

Delaney: *Yeah!*

Jack: *What do I do?*

Delaney: *Pretend you're an alien and trying to take out my rocket ship.*

Jack: *Okay, got it!*

For the next hour, they played this scenario out, swerving through the galaxy, playing cat and mouse and getting thrown into galactic jail cells.

My first thought: *What in the hell are these people doing?*

My second thought: *Sigh . . . I remember those days.*

There was a time when we had bold, crazy visions of whom we could become.

I polled the kids in my home. At the time of writing, they are ages: 13, 11, 10, 8, and 7.

13-year old: *Professional basketball player*

11-year old: *Baker*

10-year-old: *Businessman*

8-year-old: *Firefighter*

7-year-old: *Godzilla*

What you can't see from reading this book was the glossy excited look in their eyes and faces when I asked, "Who do you want to be when you grow up." Notice that I asked them *who* and not *what*. *What* is a terminal destination. *Who* evokes evolution. I could sense them scanning the CPUs of their little brains, surveying the coolest things they had seen and done, and plucking the best possible future for themselves.

What Happened?

So what happened to us? How did we slip into this adulting malaise? Here are a few suspects:

We encountered setbacks.

We accumulated mortgages.

We listened to naysayers.

And somewhere in our lives, we started "playing it safe." It is easy to take gambles when you're broke. When I sent those letters to 32 NFL teams, all of them but one passed on the opportunity to take in a law school grad whose last days of playing football were in high school. But when Coach Edwards called from Kansas City with a training camp internship offer, I could say yes without hesitation. Why? First, it was the only coaching offer on the table. Second, I wasn't responsible for anyone but me. The decision to jump into my beat-up Tahoe and trek from Cambridge to Kansas City was made easier by the fact that no one (but me) would starve if I hit absolute rock-bottom. I was single, childless, and broke—a cocktail that pairs well with risk-taking.[2]

As we climb the age ladder, our carry-on luggage gets heavier. We pick up experiential baggage as we learn that life is nonlinear by design. There isn't a logical if-then progression to life, and many of our projections don't pan out.

LIFE IS NONLINEAR
BY DESIGN.

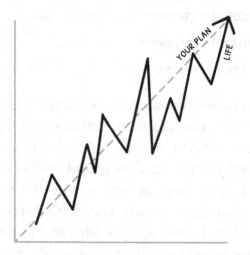

In my high school journal, I wrote the following:

- Go to Univ. of Texas
- Student body president
- Go to Harvard Law School
- Practice in Houston
- Come back to MP and start law firm
- Run for state senate
- Run for governor[3]

I had the next 30 years of my life mapped out and I was convinced I'd be governor of Texas by age 40. Well, at the time of writing, I am 45 years old and not writing this from the governor's mansion.[4]

One thing I learned in the NFL is that a play never turns out the way that you draw it up. As a quality control coach my first two seasons, I spent hours on hours drawing plays. I drew coverages. I drew blitzes. I drew runs. I drew passes. I was the Black Bob Ross minus the afro and canvas.

In my seven years of coaching, I never saw a play develop the same way that I drew it on the board. Not once. The neat 90-degree lines and precise arrows. The parallel pass routes and intersection line stunts. None of it unfurled how I drew it on paper. And there's a simple explanation for this divergence: humans do what humans do. When 22 humans start moving around with their own intentions, scripts break down.

If our plans are predrawn plays, then life is what happens when the whistle blows. Things change quickly, and in what seems like a short span of time, a decade can pass before our eyes.

Complacency Is the Enemy

To win the war against complacency, you must know your enemy. In our quest to become fuller versions of ourselves, the enemy is the status quo. This is the current version of ourselves. It's a composite of our habits, hopes, and relationships over an extended period of time. For our purposes, we'll do a six-month lookback. A 180-day snapshot gives us a large enough sample size to assess where we stand in three categories: work, family, and health.

So be honest. How is life going? Where are the pain points? Where is the friction? Where is the light? What is holding you back? What roadblocks litter the path between where you are and where you want to be?

Embrace Beta

Beta represents the constant of change that is built into the equation of life. Just think of how many predictions about your life that you were dead wrong about. Let that sink in for a moment: No one *should* be able to see your future better than you, and even you have been wrong about your fate.

There are cities that we were certain would amaze us and they didn't. There are promotions we knew we would get, but we didn't. And there were people we thought were essential to have in our lives, but alas, we've survived without them. The next moment, let alone the future, is an infinite web of decision trees. Instead of fighting outcomes, let's engender a spirit of slowing down and acknowledging that at the very least, change is an indicator that we're alive.

What Lights Me Up?

I am an urban gardener.[5] While growing up in East Texas, I would watch my dad tend to the small garden we had in our backyard. He grew up in a time and place when people *had to* farm. It wasn't something you did for Instagram.[6] No one was recording as you planted your corn or thumped watermelons to see if they were ripe. Farming literally put food on the table.

But for us, it was a recreational venture. I'd help him plant collards and mustards, radishes, and tomatoes. I'd watch slender flags of green shoot out of the earth, marking where onions were buried. Although I enjoy every second I spend in my garden today, I didn't appreciate the time that I spent in those gardens in my hometown of Mount Pleasant. Let me be clear. I wasn't rising at dawn and breaking the ground with my bare hands. This was not onerous work (although inwardly I'd convince myself that it was). But spending time in the garden meant I had less time to spend with my Nintendo. There were new levels of Zelda to conquer, so I was always thankful to hear my Dad say, "Time to go in."

I am certain that you have some similar experience to mine. Some task or chore or perhaps an "imposed hobby" that bored you in your youth but thrills you in adulthood. Nearly 30 years later, one can find me somewhere in the backyard. Hands and knees in dirt, inspecting the base of an okra plant. Or taking my shovel to a bin of compost, smelling the aroma of orange peels mixed with dead leaves.

One day I was schlepping about in the garden. I could hear my children playing in the front yard when a man walked up and asked if their father was home.

My first thought: these solar panel merchants are relentless.

My second thought: I wonder what my kids will say.

My eldest daughter piped up, "Don't knock on the door, he's probably in the back playing with plants."

Well, she was right. The soil is my refuge of solace. I make time for it because the reluctant tomato plants, uncompromising weeds, and overzealous blackberry vines bring me joy. They light me up.

Now, here's a question for you: what lights you up?

Close your eyes, (I'm serious), and pause this audiobook, close the book, or put down your Kindle and audibly ask yourself, *What lights me up?*

What is the thing that you do when you don't have to do anything? What inhabits those sparsely populated stretches of unencumbered and uninterrupted time? I'm talking about the thing that no one has to force you to do. Not your boss. Not your partner. Not your child. Just you. If you allow yourself to sit with this thing (or things) for a while, to take in the feeling of doing the thing, I bet you'll find two qualities: (1) you can't get enough of it and (2) you don't do it enough.

This is a time to prioritize you. Consider this introspection to be a form of self-care. Self-care is not a luxury; it is a necessity.

Deep Dive: What Lights Me Up?

List three to five activities that you wish you had more time for. Don't judge them based on your proficiency; rather, tap into the raw emotions that you feel when you're doing the thing.

What are the activities that make your belly tingle?

_____

_____

_____

_____

_____

_____

_____

_____

_____

_____

_____

_____

_____

_____

_____

_____

_____

_____

4

Principle 4: Wiretap Your Mental Chatter

That space between our ears is the birthplace for
conversations that shape who we believe we can become.
Let's listen and examine the voices in our head.

Welcome to the FBI

After I left the coaching world in 2013, I went through an
identity crisis. For seven years, I had attached my worth to a
logo. For me, being associated with the NFL shield was not
just a convenient conversation starter. It was a refuge. If
I met someone, I was confident that our conversations
would hover over the menial. They'd ask annoying questions

like had I ever met Tom Brady or Peyton Manning. They'd ask whether they could get tickets to an upcoming game. They'd comment on how "cool" it must be to work in the league. I wore that mask for so long that I internalized the shield. I had a full-blown case of logo delusion disorder (LDD). LDD is a condition that affects the majority of working humans and is characterized by confusing one's identity and value with an employer.

As I contemplated my next move, nothing felt right. I would imagine a new future, and quickly dismiss it. So, I started eavesdropping on my mental chatter. I imagined myself as one of those agents in the Mafia movies, headphones on while writing notes. I listened to my "self-talk" and noticed the voice I used with my kids and wife differed in tenor from the voice I used with myself. As I talked with my kids, I spoke softly (most of the time). I slowed my tempo. I blunted the edges. But when I talked to myself, I threw on my Samuel L. Jackson hat.[1] As I explored options for the next stage in my life, I thought of all the potential roadblocks:

I need another degree.
I don't have enough contacts.
No one is going to invest in this.

We've discussed how our brains are wired to keep us safe. It should come as no surprise that when a go-for-broke opportunity or chance to take a risk comes our way, that ball of mush in our heads turns up the "It won't work." frequency and turns down the, "F#*k it. Let's figure it out!" levels. Here's what it sounds like:

There's no way I could do that.
She's smarter. That's why she can do it and I can't.
You can't start a business; you didn't go to business school.

Self-Defeating Stories

A self-defeating story (SDS) is a narrative that conjures a person's previous (1) setback or (2) feeling of impostor syndrome. An SDS grows out of an episode that we tend to view as unfavorable. Things didn't go the way we had planned, so our brain takes the raw material from that experience and manufactures a self-defeating story. Here are a few examples from my life to illustrate the types of origin stories of my loudest self-defeating stories.

In 1996, I had "slightly" above-average athletic skills as a high school football player. During a spring workout of my junior year, our defensive coordinator walked up to me and said, "You're our starting safety this fall. Get ready." On the outside I was all smiles. On the inside, well, that was a different matter. I was scared. I thought about how undersized I was. How I had average speed and quickness.

In 2000, I won a tightly contested race to become student government president at the University of Texas. After running and winning, I walked into my office, closed the door, and cried. They weren't merely tears of joy. I was downright scared. Did I actually win? Did we need a recount? Was I ready for this stage?

In 2004, I looked up at a painting of Oliver Wendell Holmes in Langdell Hall. It was my first day of law school.

The previous four years were spent languishing on the wait list. Did the Harvard Law School Admissions Committee make a mistake?

In 2008, my defensive coordinator Gunther Cunningham yelled, "Get in here already!" He held the door open for me to walk into my first defensive coaches meeting. My body temp had to be 221. I kept thinking, "But, wait. I'm not really a coach!"

The self-defeating story has its roots in unworthiness and it thrives on disbelief. Unworthiness wants to convince us that we don't deserve the gift. The job. The relationship. The promotion. Disbelief corroborates the narrative by chiming in with our deficits. It feeds the tale with scraps from our "failures." To beat self-defeating stories, follow the game plan described in the next sections.

THE SELF-DEFEATING STORY IS ROOTED IN UNWORTHINESS.

Make a U-Turn

Dr. Kristin Neff is a former colleague of mine from the University of Texas. After earning her PhD from the University of California at Berkeley, she did a two-year stint at the University of Denver for postdoctoral study. She began researching self-concept development. Her research on self-compassion has influenced many of my daily internal practices related to self-talk. In describing self-compassion, she writes, "Self-compassion simply involves doing a U-turn and giving yourself the same compassion you'd naturally show a friend when you're struggling or feeling badly about yourself. It means being supportive when you're facing a life challenge, feel inadequate, or make a mistake. Instead of just ignoring your pain with a "stiff upper lip" mentality or getting carried away by your negative thoughts and emotions, you stop to tell yourself 'this is really difficult right now; how can I comfort and care for myself in this moment?'"[2]

It is easy for us to spring into action when we feel the people in our corner need our support. For example, think of when a loved one gets rejected. Immediately we shower them with supportive language. We tell them their self-worth is not dependent on a college acceptance or degree. We paint pictures of how their life will turn out wonderfully without being a part of the school that rejected them. We rush to shore up their self-worth.

Now, think through how we talk to ourselves in the same situation. I can remember when I received that first wait-list letter from Harvard Law School. I was devastated.

Immediately, I turned to my numerical performance—GPA and LSAT scores. Clearly I wasn't smart enough, because I would have scored higher on both and would have been accepted.

Then I turned to my personal statement from my application for admission. I reread it and found one punctuation error. I was disgusted with myself. How could I have missed that comma where there should have been a period. A Harvard-trained lawyer would never make a mistake like this.

What compounded my self-devaluing was that I knew two other people who had been admitted to Harvard Law School. I had been in several classes with them. I replayed all of their in-class commentary from the previous four years. Yep, *they were* smarter.

Notice how our inner selves are quick to critique and compare when we face rejection. Remember that U-turn that Dr. Neff described? Let's practice pumping the breaks and changing direction when the negative soundtracks grow louder.

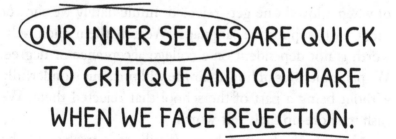

OUR INNER SELVES ARE QUICK
TO CRITIQUE AND COMPARE
WHEN WE FACE REJECTION.

The ARC Method

The first step is to **acknowledge** the presence of your SDS. Here's how I talk to my self-defeating stories: "I see you. I hear you. I honor your presence." In situations where it seems like our SDSs are spinning out of control, it is important to remember that emotions are not directions; they are indicators. The SDS wants to lurk in the far recesses of our mind, steal our drive, and embed doubt into our aspirations. Give it an audience, but not authority.

Second, we have to **resist**. Our beings and future selves need to hear us both stand up for and comfort ourselves. Think about how quickly you would come to the defense of someone you love. I don't care if it was your dog or daughter; if you thought they were being verbally assaulted, you would rush to their defense. This is the same urgency we need in the fight to control our brain.

And the final step is to **choose courage**. And *even if we don't believe the words* there is still power in saying them. I'm going to repeat that last point. Merely speaking positive words into our bodies is a brain-altering exercise. Just as smiling (in times of distress) forces the brain to release dopamine into our systems. There are very few mornings when I wake up that I want to work out instead of sleep. And so every morning, I am looking at myself in the mirror and telling my body that I am excited to work out. When self-defeating stories dominate the mental playlist, counter the song with "I am worthy. I am worthy. I am worthy."

For this chapter, I am assigning two short and important deep dives. Why? I find that learning to hug and extend grace to ourselves can be the make or break between living a life of resilience or regret.

Deep Dive 1: What's in Your Mental Playlist?

Spotify does this annoyingly amusing thing at the end of each year. The algorithms spit out data about listeners' tendencies: most listened to artists, tracks, and so on. Now, it's our turn.

What tracks play in the background of your internal conversations? These songs may seem like white noise at first, but turn up the volume and their lyrics begin to take shape.

Here, list the titles of three negative tracks that play in your head when you try to make progress or tackle a new goal.

My SDS playlist:

Track 1:

_____

_____

Track 2:

_____

_____

Track 3:

_____

_____

Deep Dive 2: The ARC

Now, here is the part where we take over the DJ's booth. The fear control center of the brain—the amygdala—is a powerful little peanut. Allowing your SDS to play on repeat feeds the amygdala. To break the cycle, you have to talk to the nut.

What are the tracks we're going to play to counter our self-defeating stories? As an example, let's take a hypothetical track and call it:

Track 1: But Your Last Business Failed

Here is an example:

"I honor your presence."
"I won't allow you to control my intentions and actions."
"I choose courage and I am worthy."

That's it! You don't have to be Bob Dylan.
Just craft your **ARC** in the following space.
Acknowledge, **resist**, and choose **courage**.

_____

_____

_____

_____

5

Principle 5: Go Small to Get Home

Give Yourself a High-Five

Look at you!

Yes, I'm talking to *you*. You did it. You made it to the fifth principle. Congrats on making it this far. To commemorate your achievement, I hope you'll join with me in singing "Chuck E's Happy Dance" song. Frankly, Chuck E. Cheese creeps me out, but as the father of five kids, I've spent more time in Chuck E. Cheese establishments than I am proud to admit.

Anyway, there's a line in the song where Chuck E. says, "And give yourself a high-five." That's right, you deserve it, damn it. Go ahead and give yourself a high-five. As you'll find out in Part II: *Mechanics*, celebrating is a critical component of the Microwins System. For some reason, the older we get, the more we think that celebrations can only take place for earth-shattering occasions. Well, get ready to channel your inner little person, because in order for us to sustain momentum and keep chipping away at our big goals, we're going to be celebrating a lot on this journey.

Where We've Been

In Principle 1: Embrace You Coffin, we tapped into our mortality. In Principle 2: Time Is Made, Not Found, we identified the importance of guarding our minutes. Our third principle, Wage War Against Your Status Quo, was a call to arms, and in Principle 4: Wiretap Your Mental Chatter, we listened in on the conversations that dominate our mental playlist.

Where We're Going

In Part II, we're going to jump into the mechanics of microwins, but before we get there, let's take some time to embrace smallness.

When I was coaching for the Detroit Lions, I coached a rookie defensive back. Let's call him Lavar Simpson. Lavar was a solid player in college. I attended his pro day right before the NFL draft. A pro day is a showcase of every draft-eligible player at a particular college or university. So, let's say for example we're talking about the University of Florida, and its football team has four players who will get drafted. Well, while four players will get drafted, there will be hundreds of players who are not drafted but are signed as free agents.

Let me get back to the story. I am attending this particular college's pro day to evaluate a certain player, when I see Lavar run onto the field. I could tell from the way he approached the first drill that this guy was serious about the task at hand. By the end of the pro day, I looked at my notebook. I had more pages of notes on Lavar than I had on the player I was actually there to see.

When I got back to Detroit, I told the defensive coordinator we needed to get the guy. We picked him up after the draft on a free agency contract and on the call to congratulate him, he asks me, "So, coach, what can I start working on?" I told him that I would overnight a defensive playbook to him and I wanted him to spend 10 minutes on it each day.

Him: *Ah, coach, 10 minutes is nothing.*

Me: *No, it's more than 9 minutes and less than 11.*

Him: *That's nothing, coach! I can at least hit the playbook for two maybe three hours a day.*

Me: *Nope. Start with 10 minutes.*

How many times have you heard, "Go big or go home!"? It's a mantra with indiscernible roots. Urban legend claims that a motorcycle parts company in Southern California coined the phrase in a 1990s sales campaign. Others claim the term grew out of surfing culture.[1] Regardless of the phrase's origin story, it has been a rallying cry for the past few decades. Whether on your Little League softball team or before a Q1 kickoff, I'm sure you've heard the term used as motivating language.

Take a moment to think about what our society is really communicating when we say *Go big or go home*. We create a 0-1 dynamic. Either we go over the top and exhaust our energy to expand our action to its physical limits, or it's a failure. Not only does this mindset set a person up for disappointment but it also creates a false dichotomy. On the spectrum of success there is a range of options that lie between "big" and "home." Also, note how this mindset primes our bodies to ignore the beauty of small wins.

The Microwins System shuns the hustlenista movement. For the majority of my life, I've been a proud card-carrying member of the hustlenistas. I preached the tenets of "grind" culture. I was the kind of guy who would scoff if someone said they woke up at any time later than 4:30 a.m.[2] I bought into the notion that the only way I could make meaningful progress on my goals was to lose sleep, weight, and my sanity in the process.

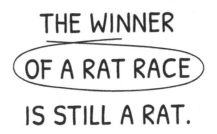

THE WINNER
OF A RAT RACE
IS STILL A RAT.

Minimum Detectable Progress

But imagine a world in which you focus on the small victories, those barely discernible victories. On the path to the monumental lies the markers of the menial. If your goals are big and difficult enough, they will take time. How much time? Well, we've already discussed how humans are really bad at making time projections, so let's just assume that it's going to take more time than we think it's going to take. What's going to keep us going? What will prevent us from giving up?

Minimum detectable progress shifts the emphasis from the shiny end product to today's small work. In the startup world, minimum viable product (MVP) describes a program that has just enough functionality and features for a user to tinker with the product. It is exactly what its name suggests, *minimal*. Instead of spending a lot of time and resources building out every single feature, the founding team decides to create a primitive prototype.

This can be a tough task for founders, namely because pride rears its ugly head quite early in the innovation process. During my time at the University of Texas, I taught a business school course on innovation, created the Center for Sports Leadership & Innovation, and served as a partner with a hybrid venture capital and philanthropic firm. In short, I spent a lot of time around startup founders.

One of the toughest periods during the ideation process was convincing the founders to convert their earth-shifting idea into a small prototype, an MVP. One team of students wanted to build a match-making startup to connect employers with college interns. The design for the proposed website involved 10 subpages and a host of bells and whistles. I sat down with them and said three words: make it small.

They believed they had a good idea but not only did we not know if companies needed this type of service but we also had no clue whether they would actually pay for it. On my recommendation, they built a stripped down Google Form to illustrate the startup and sent it to a couple of hundred companies. We quickly found out that the market didn't want what we thought it did. The founders had saved themselves from building a business that wouldn't have any customers.

The End in Mind and the Now in Focus

You can start with the end in mind, but you must live with the now in focus. Emily Dickinson wrote a poem entitled, "Forever—is composed of Nows." Take a moment to think about that, the totality of our lives is nothing more than a collection of small moments. We are a walking stack of snapshots. Sure, looking into a hopeful future to conjure an image of who we want to become is important. What will take us from who we are to who we want to be is a consistent stacking of small wins.

I'll give you an example. Today, I consistently meditate for 365 days a year. My sessions last for no more than 10 minutes. During the quarantine in 2020, I started searching for anything to help me survive. I was thankful that my family of seven was not experiencing health issues. I knew friends and loved ones who not only became sick but also died from COVID. I needed something to latch onto, and so I returned to a practice that I had struggled to maintain: meditation.

During law school, I had a next door neighbor who was a yogi to the core. We struck up a friendship, and I asked him why he was always so calm? He was a PhD student and I couldn't understand why he wasn't as stressed as every other grad student that I knew was. I figured it was the yoga.

"Oh, the calmness comes from meditation, not the yoga. The yoga definitely helps but I owe any semblance of sanity to meditation," he said.

I was sold. Sitting on his couch one Saturday afternoon, I took five pages of notes on the practice. I asked for book recommendations. I attended a few workshops on campus. I bought incense, candles, and a mat. I illegally downloaded Gregorian chants. I even sat with him for a few sessions. But you know what?

Within three months, I had discarded all of the meditation paraphernalia and gone back to my stress-led life.

When I revisited the practice in May 2020, I crafted a microwin to get started:

- Meditate for 30 minutes.

Then, I revised the goal:

- Meditate for 20 minutes.

Finally, I decided to set myself up for a no-failure situation. I merely wrote:

- Sit in closet for one minute.

My alarm went off at 4:45 a.m. the next morning and I jumped out of bed and rushed to my closet. I whipped out my wife's yoga mat and took a seat. With the giddiness of a child descending the stairs on Christmas morning, I crossed my legs, closed my eyes and breathed in deeply . . .

I did it again.

And again.

I did it a few more times.

The alarm I set went off, I stood up and walked out of the closet.

Each week, it felt good to place a "check" beside my meditation microwin. The simplicity of just one minute slowly grew into 5 minutes, and then 10. Now, I consistently get 30 minutes of quality meditation every single day.

Own the Process: Make It Yours

As we move forward into the mechanics of the system, I hope my meditation story encourages you to go as small as you need to go and own the process. The world is brimming with experts for every human pain point. There is a TikTok personality ready to sell you on the best solution to solve _____ (insert problem here).

I believe that we own the building blocks to the solutions that plague us. Instead of submerging ourselves into a deluge of "expert opinions" let's take ownership of both the challenge and the solution.

Blips over Blimps

And when it comes to crafting microwins, size matters. After identifying our macrowins (more on this process in Chapter 6), we're going to drill farther and farther into the heart of our big goal until we uncover a microwin that we're almost guaranteed to accomplish. If you were to share this microwin with other people, it might sound a little silly. People on the outside of this system crave big splashes.

We are concerned, however, with momentum. These small daily accomplishments won't make sense to a lot of people in your circle, but stick with it. I can remember telling a college buddy about one of my health microwins. At the time, the microwin was drink one green smoothie.

My buddy said, "So you're taking it easy, huh?" I'll be honest, the remark rubbed me the wrong way. But then I remembered *who* I was doing this for. I knew that drinking a green smoothie each morning would give me the momentum to make better eating decisions the rest of the day.

And those days would grow into weeks and months. If I stayed the course, not only would I feel better but also my health would improve. I'd maximize my chances of living long enough to meet and enjoy my grandkids. It is tempting to belittle the tiny victories we amass each day. But, fret not, these victories will crystallize into positive results in the future.

Deep Dive: How Small Can You Go?

First, think about a scary goal that you've always wanted to accomplish. Now, answer this question: what would a small step look like on the path to grasping that big goal? Write it here:

_____

_____

_____

_____

Okay, now, break that step down into a smaller slice. For example if the scary goal was, "write a book," then maybe your small slice could be, "write 10 pages" or "create list of chapters."

_____

_____

_____

_____

You guessed it. We're not done yet! Keep going. Break that goal down until we need a microscope to see it! Using our example, let's turn "write 10 pages" into "write one page." We would turn "create list of chapters" into "write the first sentence of the introduction."

_____

_____

_____

_____

I know this is tedious work. Your brain is probably telling you that these small units of work aren't worth chasing, but keep believing that you are building the blueprint for a seismic shift in your life, because you are.

II

Mechanics

Now, it's time for strategy. This is the part of the book where we get down to the nitty-gritty of the Microwins System. In *Mechanics*, our focus shifts to movement.

Here is a brief summary of the chapters in this part:

Chapter 6: Macrowins

Macrowins are bold and force us to reimagine our impact in this world. They serve as the guiding light for our daily microwins. In this chapter, you'll learn how to build macrowins from the inside out.

Chapter 7: The Three Domains

Three domains: work, family, and health are critical to building a wholehearted and meaningful life. In this chapter, we'll explore their interconnectedness and examine how we can bring them into alignment.

Chapter 8: Work

Whether you're a career employee, side crafter, or somewhere in between, this chapter will help you to unpack how you desire to see your life's work manifest itself in the world.

Chapter 9: Family

This chapter may surprise you. When we talk about family, we move beyond the confines of bloodlines and DNA. In this chapter, we will shore up your relationships to the living world around you.

Chapter 10: Health

Is there anything more important than health? The nature of this domain tends to spill over into the other parts of life. Thus, we are going to apply a special brand of focus and intentionality to charting our approach to health.

Chapter 11: The Microwins System

With the building blocks in place, there is just one last thing to do: go!

CHAPTER

6

Macrowins

It's time for that ambitious, sprite, idealistic version of you (who you've been suppressing for the past five chapters) to come out and play. We've extolled the virtues of going small. And now, as we lay the foundation of the Microwins System, it's time to go big.

First, give yourself some credit. You did a lot of hard and heavy lifting in the *Mindset* section of this book. Many of those deep dives asked you to tap into a level of vulnerability that may have felt uncomfortable. Thinking about one's own death is an emotionally taxing thought experiment. But, *you* did the work and if you're reading this section, then you've separated yourself from the vast majority of people who start self-help books. Most of them ditch the text and revert to their status quo before reaching the book's midpoint. You've reached the point of no return. *Keep going*. Let's talk about macrowins.

What Is a Macrowin?

I can hear you saying, "Is this a typo? I thought this book was about *micro*wins."

This book *is* about microwins, but let's take a step back for a moment. Microwins are small units of victory that feed into big goals. The question arises, "Well, what are those big goals?" That's where macrowins come in.

Remember when you learned about prefixes and suffixes back in grade school? If not, don't worry. The prefix *macro* is a derivative of the Greek word *makr*, meaning "long, tall, high, or large." Therefore, a *macrowin* is a bawdy aspirational goal.

Remember previously in the book when I asked you to imagine your own funeral? You took an introspective look into what you wanted to be remembered for. You imagined the impact that you could have on others. Well, macrowins are the North Star that guides us to that destination. No, macrowins don't hasten death.[1] They have the opposite effect. Macrowins should take you to a time and place where you felt unencumbered by other people's thoughts of you.

I asked a question previously in the book that I hope you remember. It's the same question that I like to ask people who are struggling with finding purpose and meaning in their lives: who were you going to be before the experts got involved? Think about it. At some point in your life, you felt free. It seemed like the world was an oyster of opportunity. You could be and do anything, or at least that's the way it felt.

But then something happened. The farther you marched through the educational system and adolescence, things started to change. A few years ago, I was giving a speech in Los Angeles. My usual practice is to stick around after my keynotes for as long as possible so that I can talk with as many attendees as possible. Not only do those conversations help me to hone my message but I've also found those interactions to be some of the most invigorating conversations that I have.

Well, on this particular day, I had to race to LAX because I needed to get back to Austin to catch my son's last basketball game. So, as soon as the crowd started clapping, I waved and headed for backstage. In one motion, I grabbed my roller bag and confirmed a Lyft for the airport.

As I was speeding through the hotel lobby, I heard someone yelling my name, and when I turned around, I saw a noticeably frazzled gentleman running toward me. I could tell from the lanyard hanging from his neck that he had attended the speech.

To be honest, my first thought was, "Oh, Lord, this guy had a problem with something that I said in there." As the man approached me, I told him, "I really wish I could stay, but I have to run to get to the airport. My flight leaves soon."

His response floored me, "Do you mind if I ride with you?"

Yes, I did mind, but I could tell from the look on his face that he really wanted to talk and he wasn't giving any creepy vibes, so I said, "Your call. The car's pulling up now."

So, here I am, sitting in the back of a Hyundai Elantra with a guy I just met (let's call him Steve) headed to the airport.

Him: *Mr. Roberts, I enjoyed the speech. I follow you on LinkedIn.*

Me: *I appreciate the kind words. At first I thought you were hunting me down to disagree with a point that I made.*

Him: *Well, you were kinda right.*

Me: *Oh, no.*

Him: *So, you said something about it never being too late to call an audible. Look, I'm 53; my wife and I have three kids. The oldest just started her master's degree and the other two are still in high school. I'm up to my neck in bills and saving for college. How can I call an audible with all of this baggage?*

Me: *Well, who do you want to be in this life?*

Him: *Huh?*

Me: *Who do you want to be in this life?*

Him: *Well, I don't really know. I just know I can't stand working for _____. These people are nuts.*

Me: *Maybe you should start there.*

I think a lot of people can identify with Steve. We know we are unhappy in our current state. We wallow in a shallow state of being. It's surface level. Unhappiness is not a root cause; it's a symptom. The positive and negative states of happiness are surface level structures.

But in the deep end, the level far below the surface where there is very little visibility, this is where the source of our happiness lies. And what I've found is that most people are unwilling to go deep enough in order to excavate the root cause. On the ocean's floor lies an anchor that will not shake loose until you yank it free. Instead of strapping on our scuba diving gear (the five principles) and diving into the darkness, we complain. We sulk. We note every shortcoming and missed opportunity.

THE GAP BETWEEN WHO YOU ARE AND WHO YOU WANT TO BE IS EITHER AN OBSTACLE OR AN OPPORTUNITY.

Well, let's be clear. This is it. This thing we call life is brittle and comes with an expiration date. Choose the hard work and create macrowins worthy of your existence. Unless you've been reincarnated, you cannot say with certainty that you get another shot to create the life you desire. This is our chance to get it right.

The Bawdy Test

If you've worked in the corporate arena or stumbled into a business class, there is a good chance you've heard of BHAG: big hairy audacious goals. James C. Collins and Jerry I. Porras crafted this idea in the book, *Built to Last: Successful Habits of Visionary Companies*. In it, they write, "Like the moon mission, a true BHAG is clear and compelling and serves as a unifying focal point of effort—often creating immense team spirit. It has a clear finish line, so the organization can know when it has achieved the goal; people like to shoot for finish lines. A BHAG engages people—it reaches out and grabs them in the gut. It is tangible, energizing, highly focused. People 'get it' right away; it takes little or no explanation."[2]

Collins and Porras explored the successful habits of visionary companies, but let's take this approach and apply it to our personal lives. What should a macrowin look like? Where do we start in order to craft one?

We start with the BAWDY Test. BAWDY stands for (1) bright, (2) aspirational, (3) worth it, (4) delusional, and (5) why not? Let's walk through each feature.

Bright

Steve was so dissatisfied with his status quo that he was willing to skip a work conference and ride with me to the airport. He was in search of a fix. The more we talked, the more I understood that he was looking for a quick solution to his unhappiness. Nothing in his professional life gave him joy.

Macrowins should be bright. Remember back in Chapter 3, "Wage War Against Your Status Quo," I asked what lights you up? Well, hopefully you spent some intentional time and energy working through the deep dive and writing down the things that give you that spark.

That thing that brings light to your being is what the world needs more of. The earth is at capacity with people who are going through the motions. Take a look around. Do the people you observe seem to be enjoying their lives? I spend most of the day in coffee shops around Austin, Texas, and it is rare to see someone smiling. Even when they pick up their oversized cup of liquified sugar, they still have a look of unhappiness on their face.

The world needs your light. As you craft your macrowins, don't shirk from that glow. Your survival instincts will tell you:

I'm too old.
It's too late.
I'm not ready.

You're not too old and it's not too late and no one is ever ready for a life shift. I know that it can be scary to memorialize the visions we have. Yet, if not now, then when? And if not you, then who?

IF NOT <u>NOW</u>, THEN WHEN?
IF NOT <u>YOU</u>, THEN WHO?

Aspirational

An aspirational macrowin envisions us not as who we are, but who we want to become. It should be a new thing. Perhaps, you've been dabbling around the edges of this particular goal without making any meaningful headway. I like to think of a macrowin not just as a North Star, but as the entire sky. It is where we will look when the monotony of daily microwins starts to wear on us. It is the place where we will find solace and renew that tingle in the belly.

Worth It

In a previous life, I played a lot of blackjack. I had a group of law school buddies who also enjoyed the game. This shared love prompted us to take frequent trips to the Foxwoods Resort Casino during our third and final year in Cambridge. There's something called a BAR loan in which a bank lender would loan third-year students money for the costs of examination prep courses and living expenses. For the bank, it was a great deal. They were loaning money to people who were likely going to make a high salary within 6 to 12 months. For me, it was an incredible deal, and I used the cash flow to fund two activities: international travel and blackjack.

One of my good buddies used the exact same strategy every time we walked into the casino. He would get his chips, take a seat and place all of his chips on the table for his first hand. The first time I witnessed him do this, I asked him, "Are you okay?"

His response: "Yep, gotta make sure the trip is worth it."

Let me be very clear, I'm not encouraging you to pick up blackjack. What I am nudging you to do is craft macrowins that are worth it. Your game is a high-stakes affair; a lot is riding on it. Go big. Make sure your macrowin is worth it to you. Put some skin in the game.

Delusional

My favorite law school professor, David Wilkins, taught a course on professional responsibility, but the course transcended legal ethics. In every class, Wilkins forced us to grapple with who we wanted to be in life beyond the confines of a legal career.

On the last day of class, he asked us to go around the table and share our post-graduation plans. The first girl says, "I'll be clerking for Judge so-and-so on the 9th Circuit of Appeals."

You may not be a lawyer, and perhaps it's been some time since you learned about the federal court system so let me provide some context. There are 13 federal circuits that feed cases into the United States Supreme Court. It's *extremely* difficult to nab a clerkship with one of these courts.

Well, by the time my turn came around, people had mentioned Goldman Sachs, the White House, and the top firm in the country, Wachtell, Lipton, Rosen & Katz as their next destinations. Finally, it was my turn and I said, "I'll be a training camp intern with the Kansas City Chiefs." Everyone looked at me with blank stares. For a few seconds, I felt like I was on the witness stand confessing to a crime. Professor Wilkins nodded and said, "That's excellent,

Daron, I'm excited for you," and the announcements from my classmates continued.

As I was walking out of class, the "clerkship girl" ran up to me and said, "I'm not sure what you said in there, but it seems like you're going to have more fun than I am."

I told her about my summer experience and my dream of becoming a head coach in the NFL and once again, I felt like I was on the witness stand.

Did you play in the pros? Did you play in college? Is your dad a coach?

After I muttered a few nos, she flatly said, "You're crazy," and walked away.

Let's apply a slight reframing to *crazy* and call it *delusional*. One of the best features of a macrowin is that it will probably not make sense to the people around you. There's a simple reason for this. Most of the people in your circle are acquainted with past versions of you, and that history will color their perception of who you can become.

And guess what? There is nothing you can (or should) do to shift other people's perception of you. As my former head coach, Herm Edwards would say, "Control the controllables." Redirect attention away from other people's perception of you and instead, channel that energy into reimagining your future. As I found after I finally got my first NFL coaching contract, the same people who doubted you before you did it will congratulate you after it's done.

Why Not?

And finally, we come to the last feature of macrowins: why not?

In 2009, Simon Sinek delivered his first TED Talk at the TEDxPugetSound in Seattle. The title seemed fairly straightforward, "How Great Leaders Inspire Action." At the time of writing this book, the talk has garnered 64,288,210 views on TED.com. I would estimate that the speech (or excerpts of his talk) have been viewed at least 100 million times when you factor in clips that appear on social media and YouTube.

A single phrase from that speech, "Start with WHY," catapulted Sinek into the pantheon of self-help thought leaders.

As you cultivate your macrowins, I want you to end with *why not*.

Why not you?
Why not your dream?
Why not this moment?
Why not your fitness goals?
Why not your family?
Why not your business?

As you're asking yourself why not, remember Principle 4 in the *Mindset* section of this book. Put those mythical headphones over your ears and listen to your mental chatter. Our brain will rifle through our past to replay our pits before it shows us our peaks.

START WITH <u>WHY</u>,
BUT ALWAYS END WITH
WHY NOT?

You are your peaks. The dips and valleys were merely training grounds for the next climb. Now, it's time to dive into the three domains where we'll craft the macrowins and microwins to propel us forward.

Deep Dive

Take one aspect of your life (work, family, or health) and craft a macrowin. Don't get distracted by your brain telling you how long it could take you to achieve it. Push through the noise. Remember, the five features: (1) bright, (2) aspirational, (3) worth it, (4) delusional, and (5) why not? of macrowins and build away.

_____

_____

_____

_____

_____

_____

_____

_____

_____

_____

Scan the following QR code to download microwins resources and join the movement.

SCAN CODE TO JOIN THE
MICROWINS MOVEMENT

WWW.MICROWINS.CO

7

The Three Domains

Let me tell you a story that I don't share that often. After I was fired from the Cleveland Browns and before I moved my family to Austin, Texas, there was a painful five-month period of my life. I knew the right decision for our family unit was for me to leave the coaching world. I never saw my family. A lot of people have a warped sense of professional coaches. They think that we just show up with our players on Sunday afternoons, get through a game, and then show back up the next Sunday to do it all over again. This couldn't be farther from the truth.

Coaching philosophies are the root system of coaching trees. A head coach gets mentored by another head coach who was mentored by a head coach. You get the point. Systems get passed down from one generation of coaches to the next such that many of the practices that current coaches use are actually close derivatives (if not carbon copies) of systems that their coaching forefathers adopted. This doesn't just involve defensive and offensive philosophies. No, the mindsets permeate every facet of the organization.

Because the margin of victory is so low in the National Football League, every decision counts. How long rest periods will be after a game to what food should be served in pregame meals seem like colossal decisions. And in truth, they are. Oftentimes, you'll hear leaders talk about doing the "little things right." Although I understand their reasoning, I believe the terminology is misguided. When you operate in a highly pressurized and chaotic environment, there is no such thing as a little thing. The little things are big things.

MONUMENTAL THINGS
OFTENTIMES MASQUERADE
AS MENIAL.

One area of coaching that has been the slowest to change is the "guard your desk" mentality. I remember the first night that I started interning with the Chiefs. After dinner, all of the coaches showered, and instead of putting on normal clothes (jeans, shirts, etc.) I noticed that everyone was putting on their Chiefs gear (sweatpants, hoodies, etc.). And instead of walking out to the parking light, the entire staff headed upstairs and went back into their offices.

At the time, I didn't have an office. I used the coaches meeting room as my home base. So, I pulled up some film from the previous season and began watching a few clips. By 9 p.m., I finally worked up the courage to walk into the defensive quality control coach's office, Geoff Ketchum.

Me: *Hey, Ketch, how's it going?*

Ketch: *Good, what's up?*

Me: *I'm just wondering what time people start leaving.*
Ketch, reclined back in his chair, looked at the ceiling and bellowed a laugh that I feared would invite other coaches to come in and see what was going on.

Me: *C'mon, man. That was not a funny question. What's the deal?*

Ketch walked to the board and wrote "Head Coach" at the top. Beneath that, he drew three lines, each pointing to the three coordinators on our team: offense, defense, and special teams. Then he drew lines to the assistant coaches underneath each coordinator.

Ketch: *Here's the deal. Nobody, and I do mean nobody, leaves before the head coach. Once his car pulls out of the parking lot, it's open season, and the coordinators might leave. As soon as your coordinator leaves, then you're free to go. But* (and this is where he lowered his glasses and looked into my eyes), *never, ever ask to go home. Just wait until you see them walking down the hallway.*

Me: *Got it.*

Ketch: *Remember, never ask.*

As we moved from training camp into the preseason and finally into the regular season, the departure time of both the head coach and my defensive coordinator became later and later. Ten p.m. turned into midnight. What Ketch *didn't* explain to me was that if the head coach left and my defensive coordinator chose to stick around, I still had to wait until he left until I could go home.

Now, at that time, I was 29 years old. I was single. I didn't have any kids. Moreover, I didn't have anywhere to go. Without much money, I camped out at night in the basement of Arrowhead. As soon as Gunther Cunningham would leave the building, I'd go downstairs, steal some Pop Tarts from the kitchen pantry, and slink into my cave. The "cave" was a deserted meeting room. I'd inflate my Coleman twin mattress, throw a pillow and sheet down, and get four to five hours of sleep before it was time to do it again. I felt like the Black version of Bill Murray in *Groundhog Day*.[1]

This scenario played out on every team that I worked for: the Chiefs, Lions, Mountaineers, and Browns. Everyone perched at the bottom and middle tiers of the org chart waited for the cascade of departures to unfold before they dared to leave the building.

Imagine keeping this routine for seven years. Not only were the hours long, but also vacation and sick days were nonexistent. Sure, we would get a week or two off at the end of the season, and a few weeks in the summer, but that time hardly made up for the 18-hour shifts we were pulling for half of the year. During my seven years of coaching, I never witnessed a coach take a sick day. Think about that. I worked with just over 100 coaches during my career, and I never saw any of them not show up for a day of work.

This system of "guard your desk" formed the cornerstone of our approach to the work. Thus, when I found myself out of a job in 2013 and tried to repair my relationship with my wife and children, I went into a deep depression. My daily system was off. I couldn't sleep past 4 a.m. I couldn't fall asleep until midnight. As soon as I committed to stepping away from coaching, job offers rolled in.

The first offer came from the defensive coordinator I worked under in Cleveland. Ray Horton took the coordinator's position with the Tennessee Titans and as soon as he signed his contract, he gave me a call.

Ray: *D, how's it going?*

Me: *It's going well, Ray. You?*

Ray: *It hasn't been announced yet, but I took the DC job with the Titans and I want you to come work with me.*

Me: (Long pause).

Ray: *D, you there?*

Me: *Yes, I'm here, Ray. The thing is . . . I took a scouting job with the Texans.*

Ray: *What?*

Me: *Yeah, I signed the contract and am heading to Houston this weekend.*

Ray: *Well, that's no problem. We can get you out of the contract.*

Me: *You know I love working with you. I just don't feel right about backing out. Rick threw me a lifeline.*

Ray: *Well, I'll keep it open for a while, in case you change your mind.*

Me: *Appreciate you, Coach.*

You read that right. After I had promised my wife that I would take some time away from football, I took a job as a scout with the Texans. Somewhere in my spirit, deep down in my gut, I knew that (1) it wasn't the right move for me and (2) I was backing out on a promise that I had made to my family. But the NFL still had a hold on me. I needed the shield. My identity was tied to the game of football.

On a Saturday, I took a direct flight from Cleveland to Houston, checked into a Springhill Suites, and started work on that following Monday.

On Thursday of that week, I walked into the general manager's office, Rick Smith, and resigned. My wife was due to fly to Houston on Saturday to start looking for houses. On Friday, I called her with the news: I quit.

I'm proud to say that 10 years later, we are still married.

The Three Domains

Everything that we do affects everything that we do. A sugary mocha in the morning causes the crash at noon. A missed soccer game three weeks ago incites a fight over the weekend. An unsuccessful sales pitch at work foments into a quiet dinner with the family.

There is no balance. The scales will never be even. Life is a topsy-turvy existence in which the scales resemble a seesaw. You could feel fulfilled in your work, but miserable at home. Your health may be in good shape, but work falls flat.

There are three key domains that inform our being in this world. Let's call them work, family, and health. Instead of thinking of them as silos nestled beside each other, let's see them for what they really are: overlapping circles. They form a classic Venn diagram.

That shaded area where the circles meet forms our core. And that core is who we are. As the quality of activity inside of each circle changes, the core changes as well. Think of the center of the earth. It is made up of molten lava. Our normal state of being on the planet appears to be relatively still. But beneath us, the core of the earth rocks and sways as the heat moves back and forth. Let's dive into each element of our core and identify where we'll focus our attention.

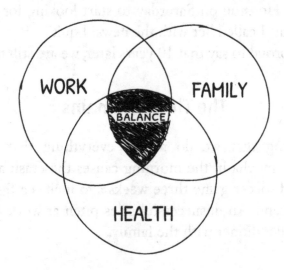

Deep Dive: #WFH

When you think of the three domains, how would you rate where you stand in each category?

Here, give each domain a score on a scale from 1 to 5 with a 1 being strongly disagree/very dissatisfied to a 5 being strongly agree/very satisfied.

How do you rate your current standing in work? _____

How do you rate your current standing in family? _____

How do you rate your current standing in health? _____

Now, think of who you want to be in 365 days. Describe the progress that you want to see using the Microwins System.

Work

_____

_____

_____

_____

Family

_____

_____

_____

_____

_____

Health

_____

_____

_____

_____

Scan the following QR code to download microwins resources and join the movement.

SCAN CODE TO JOIN THE
MICROWINS MOVEMENT

WWW.MICROWINS.CO

8

Work

What do you think of when you read the word *work*? I bet that most of you immediately think of the thing that pays your mortgage. Your mind goes to W2s or 1099s. This makes sense. After the Industrial Revolution, society transitioned from home-based work to factory-based employment. Homesteaders slowly morphed into employees.

I'm going to challenge you. As we think about work in the context of macrowins, let's expand the world of possibilities. Perhaps your W-2 gives you joy. If so, then count yourself among the lucky. Far too many Americans report being dissatisfied with their job. I'm always reminded, however, that this is not the case for everyone. I've been pulled to the side a countless number of times after keynotes by people who have told me how much they love what they do and how much they yearn to get better at it. That's a special thing. It is a rare instance when a person's livelihood lights them up.

If you're in this category of people who want to get better at your work because it lights you up, then isolate your deficiencies. Combine the feedback from your managers with deliberate self-awareness. What are the areas where you need to improve? What is the one skill in your current job that if you were to make significant improvement would alter the trajectory of your career?

Or consider an approach put forward by Daniel Shapiro, COO of LinkedIn. I had the chance to listen to Dan address the top 50 salespeople at the company. He asked a question that landed with me: What would happen if you became great in an area where you were really good? He proposed leaning into a strength and learning as much about that strength until you eventually get a little better. And then a little better. And before long your peers recognize you as the person who excels in a very discrete skill. We've all been a party to those group conversations that begin with, "Do you know of anyone who can help me with _____?" As soon as someone broaches the subject, people chime in with responses like, "Oh, I have the perfect person, their name is _____."

How do the names of these specialists percolate to the top of a conversation? Well, they get really good at something and share their expertise with the world. Some of them focused on "fixing" their deficits, but I'm convinced that most of them noticed what they enjoyed and then funneled as much of their time and attention into getting really damn good at that part of their work.

For some of you, you may find yourself in the "meh" category. You feel *okay* about your job. It's neither invigorating nor demoralizing, *it just is*. I've been there. When I first started teaching at the University of Texas, every day was a new adventure. Just driving onto campus filled me with joy. I couldn't wait for my day to begin. Walking into the classroom injected energy into my spirit. I was giddy the night before as I prepped for my lectures.

But over time, that light grew dim. I started to notice hairline fractures in my motivation. I would overhaul my syllabi, hoping that a change in content would make a difference. But it didn't. And after just shy of a decade, I left UT.

I mention this story as a reminder that we must constantly ask ourselves, What lights me up? It may seem that a lack of motivation to do our jobs is a sign that something is wrong with us. We default to blaming ourselves. Now let me be clear, I am a firm believer in accountability, but when it comes to internal motivation, the body keeps count. Rarely do our insides lie. Our educational system is built on matriculation, not development. The lock-step, check-the-box approach of advancement deposits us into college where we pick a major and hope for the best. We enter the workforce with not only a major, but a minor as well. But what we often lack is desire, a yearning to actually do the thing that we've been trained to do. I have seen this phenomenon up close as I counseled thousands of college students. The students who took my class as freshmen sat in my office as seniors. What should have been a time of celebration felt more like a period of mourning. I saw far too many students who were not excited about the next stage of their lives.

ALWAYS ASK YOURSELF THE QUESTION: WHAT LIGHTS ME UP?

So, practice some self-compassion (See Principle 4 in the *Mindset* section of this book) and extend an olive branch of grace to yourself. You are not too old and it is not too late to reclaim your life. Microwins will help us to get there.

Side Crafters

A couple of years ago, I was in San Diego delivering a keynote. Companies were slowly reverting back to hosting live events, and so I was excited to be in front of real people for a change. There was an 18-month time span when all of my talks were virtual, and let me tell you, those engagements never lit me up. If you think talking to a crowd of 500 or 1,000 people is hard, then imagine talking to a screen with 500 or 1,000 squares, many of them blackened because people chose to not share their video.

Needless to say, as I flew into California for the talk, I was excited. To be honest, I was a bit rusty and nervous but the crowd energized me. I ended my speech with the question, "What lights you up?" When I walked backstage, I accepted a few high-fives from my team and sat down. I felt like I had just completed a triathlon. I was dripping with sweat and my heart was pounding in a good way. The tingle was back. That twitch in the spine had returned. I could feel my body telling me, "Let's do more of this."

A woman walked backstage and stood in the corner. The client was a large financial firm and the CEO was reminding the team about OKRs or KPIs, and meanwhile, one of his team members was backstage staring at me.

"Daron, my name is Jessica, and I know what lights me up."

Before I could return her greeting, she started telling me about dog walking. That's right, dog walking. Even with her busy work schedule as a financial advisor, she had created a side business where she would walk other people's dogs on the weekends.

"At first, I was just walking the neighbors' dogs, but then people started asking me to do it for them as well, because of the way I talk to the dogs."

The way I talk to the dogs. This is the part of the story where I have to come clean about something. I didn't even know this industry existed until Jessica told me about it. And the more she talked, the more I watched her face light up. She couldn't stop smiling. Her pace was frenetic. She couldn't catch her breath. This weekend hobby had grown into a full-blown side business.

I also want to address another group and if my description mirrors your current state of affairs, then tune in. These people are folks that I call *people of the craft.* There is a skill they want to develop. They want to become better at coding or photography. They want to pick up videography or cake decorating. These people have had some exposure to a craft and something on the inside is telling them to chase more. That if they do more of this thing that lights them up, their life will change for the better. It may not be the thing that changes their entire life, but it may be just enough to keep them looking forward to the next day.

I want to introduce you to belly math. We live in an era that is dominated by big data. Artificial intelligence (AI) and the algorithms have dominated news headlines and captured the budgets of the world's largest companies. There isn't a day that goes by that we're not introduced to a new use for AI. But how much have you paid attention to the "little data." Little data comes from our bodies. Emotions are data, too. Sure, this form of intel doesn't show up on an Excel spreadsheet, but our bodies deserve our highest form of attention and respect. If you haven't found that work that lights you up, keep looking. Keep injecting yourself into new circles and unfamiliar places.

At one point I was coaching a mid-level executive who worked at a top-five food and beverage company. She was in the engineering side, had risen through the ranks in rapid fashion, and was the talk of the executive suite. There was just one problem: she wasn't happy. She had always done well in math and science but didn't particularly enjoy them. When I asked her what her favorite undergraduate class was, she didn't hesitate: marketing! I took this random marketing class at the business school and it was fascinating.

Me: *Great! Your homework is to find some marketing people at your company and treat them to lunch.*

Before our scheduled coaching session, she texted me: *Had lunch w/ some marketing ppl. They rock!* In three months, she had transitioned into an entry-level marketing job with her company. As it turns out, her light was on the other side of the campus and all she had to do was treat a few people to tacos.

Maybe finding what lights you up will require you to travel overseas or take a vow of silence and renounce your worldly possessions. Or, your light may be on the side of campus. No one is going to search for you. That's your job.

Deep Dive: Choose Your Own Adventure

Some of my favorite childhood books were in the "Choose Your Own Adventure" series. At the end of a chapter, the reader was given a choice. Here's an example: "If you'd like to go into the cave, turn to page 29. If you want to turn around and take the raft upstream, go to page 84."

Let's play around with some scenarios.

Let's say that you like where you work. If you could do another job function (completely different from what you are doing right now), what would it be?

_____

_____

_____

_____

_____

If you could get really good (like black belt good) at one side craft, what would it be and why?

_____

_____

_____

_____

_____

Scan the following QR code to download microwins resources and join the movement.

SCAN CODE TO JOIN THE
MICROWINS MOVEMENT

WWW.MICROWINS.CO

CHAPTER

9

Family

Clayton Christensen was an academic and best-selling author of 10 books, including the widely acclaimed *The Innovator's Dilemma*. In 2010, the graduating class at Harvard Business School asked Christensen to provide advice on how they should approach their post-graduation life. In a talk to the class, Christensen said, "People who are driven to excel have this unconscious propensity to underinvest in their families and overinvest in their careers—even though intimate and loving relationships with their families are the most powerful and enduring source of happiness."[1]

Just as we expanded the world of possibility beyond the traditional notion of *work*, we are going to apply the same principle to *family*.

First, answer this question honestly and without too much deliberation: What comes to mind when you read the word *family*?

Take some time and think.

What did you come up with? There are traditional concepts of family that encompass the people with whom we share blood ties. Your mind may have gone to your mother, brother, or an aunt. These are some of the first humans that we form bonds with as we enter the world. Beyond sharing some strands of genetic code, we also share time. Summer trips, reunions, bat mitzvahs, quinceañeras. These are the adolescent life moments that strengthen the bonds among family members.

But what about that one college buddy who has been in your corner since freshman year? The one who you never hesitate to call whether you're experiencing the best of times or the worst of times. Or how about that coworker from two jobs ago. The two of you would commiserate over the antics of Bob in accounting. Should we include them as well? Or what about your dog? The answer is yes.

Here's a question that I ask myself as I'm thinking about who my "family" is. It's going to sound simple, but give it a try: who is in my corner? In Principle 2 in the *Mindset* part of this book, we distinguished corners from circles. Circles of humans are malleable, easily formed, and oftentimes arbitrary. The other mother that you talk with while waiting in the pick-up line could be in your circle. The people from the nonprofit that you used to volunteer with might be in it as well. And high school friends that you haven't seen for 20 years (or in my case 25) could also find themselves in your circle.

But are they in your corner? The people in your corner choose to be there. They stick around when your stock is at an all-time low. They don't go missing during the pits of your life. They don't just show up when you've reached a peak.

My dad is a Baptist minister, and when I was young, I would go with him everywhere. If he went to church, I was there. If he went to the nursing home, I was with him. When he officiated weddings, I was in a pew. And when he officiated funerals, I was there.

The funerals always stood out to me because I can remember looking for people in attendance. I would notice who didn't show up. Lifelong friends who lived across town or the cousin who lived just a few miles away. Some of the people who I thought would never miss the homegoing of a loved one were not in attendance. I mention those memories as a reminder to you that it's time to double-down on your closest relationships.

I had the chance to host my good friend, Coach Buzz Williams, on my show, "This Is Not About Sports." My relationship with Buzz goes back a decade. While coaching with the Detroit Lions, a story ran about my unlikely path to the NFL in *ESPN the Magazine*. Buzz read the article and noticed that we shared a common mentor: Coach Marc McDaniel. Coach McDaniel was my high school head football coach. He is a man of few words, but he's the type of guy that who makes people get quiet when he talks. Every word is built for efficiency and impact.

Buzz worked as a high school student assistant for Coach McDaniels (in a different small Texas town) before I played for him. I received an email from Buzz suggesting that the two of us connect and we did.

Buzz said something that stuck with me, "I want to be famous in my home. I want to be my wife's best friend. I want to be the dad and husband that boys look at and say, 'Man, if I could do that every day, that'd be a great life.'"

Let that sink in for a moment.

You may or may not have children. That's beside the point. Think of what Coach Williams is saying here. He wants to live his life in such a way that his wife and children feel him. They absorb his energy. He doesn't want to merely punch the clock. Many of us have copy-pasted the corporate practice of "clocking in and clocking out" into our personal lives. We show up for the sake of showing up. Piddle around a bit. Make some noise so people around us can say that they saw us there, and then leave.

Coach Buzz has taken his desire to be the best version of a father and husband that he can be into his daily practice. He doesn't call them microwins, but Coach has a daily practice that would fit squarely into the Microwins System under "Family." He writes a letter to each one of his kids every single day. In my interview with him for my LinkedIn series, "This Is Not About Sports," he said, "So I write my children every day that they go to school. I've never missed a day. The note may be three sentences from this conversation. And tomorrow three sentences on an entirely different topic. And I don't think my children would say this to me, but what an incredible inheritance?"

As you can imagine, being a college head basketball coach is a demanding job. I worked as a college assistant coach at West Virginia University for two years, and it was five times as demanding as the National Football League. Why? In the NFL, no one calls you when you're away from the office. Now, the truth of the matter is that you are rarely away from the office, but during the brief moments of freedom, you are truly off the clock. If there is a problem with a player, it gets handled without an assistant coach's help.

Not so in college. In college, my phone was a hotline.

Jimmy didn't show up for psychology class.
Ashton is homesick.
Maverick just committed to Syracuse.

You're never "off the clock" in college. Coach Williams has every excuse to not follow through with his daily microwins of writing notes to his kids, but he still does it. He budgets the time and space every day to ensure that it gets done.

The people in your corner deserve the best of you instead of the rest of you.

THE PEOPLE IN YOUR CORNER
DESERVE THE (BEST) OF YOU
INSTEAD OF THE _REST_ OF YOU.

Deep Dive: People, Pets, and Plants

Who (or what) are two to three people, pets, and/or plants that you want to strengthen your relationship with? And no, that's not a typo. Let's include pets and plants into this equation.

PEOPLE	PETS	PLANTS

Scan the following QR code to download microwins resources and join the movement.

SCAN CODE TO JOIN THE
MICROWINS MOVEMENT

WWW.MICROWINS.CO

10

Health

Close your eyes and imagine you are lying in a hospital bed. You've been told by the doctor that you have three weeks to live. Of the three domains, which one would you do anything to get more of? Would you call your boss and beg for overtime? No, of course not. As our health declines and we get closer to death, we wish for the good health that we previously enjoyed, but likely took for granted, during earlier parts of our life. What wouldn't you do for lower blood pressure, greater lung capacity, or the ability to hike without knee pain in your elder years? Although every domain is important, health carries a special spillover effect.

Better health empowers us with the time, energy, and stamina to improve our work and pour life into our family.

Health, like finance, is one of those life categories that suffers from a phenomenon known as temporal discounting. Think of temporal discounting as the rate at which someone devalues (or minimizes) delayed rewards. I'll give you an example: When I coached I was around a lot of other coaches who "dipped." Dipping is shorthand for using chewing tobacco. I picked up the habit. Every time that I would purchase a can, I would read the warning on the front of the can, "This product contains nicotine. Nicotine is an addictive chemical." And guess what, I'd open the can, and enjoy the calming effect of letting the nicotine enter my bloodstream.

Now, if you were to stop me and say, "Daron, do you know the use of chewing tobacco could put you at risk of getting throat cancer?" And I'd say, "Yes." But guess what? I used it for years before finally kicking the habit. I knew that every single "dip" could lower the number of days that I have on this planet, and I still chose to dip because in the moment, I valued the calming effect. That's what temporal discounting can explain, choosing short-term indulgences at the expense of long-term consequences.

So, as we think about creating a macrowin for health, what comes to mind? Let's back up: when you read the word *health*, what connotations of the term emerge?

I can assume that many of you may be thinking about your weight and how many pounds you'd like to lose. Or maybe it's your diet or workout routine (or lack thereof). According to the National Institutes of Health, "the word 'health' is derived from an old English word *hale*, which means "wholeness, being whole or sound."[1]

Wholeness

Wholeness captures the state of both our physical and spiritual beings. The inputs that feed our body and soul combine to form a diet. The most common connotation of diet centers on taking things away or going without. Instead of operating from a deficit mindset, let's focus on abundance. When you think of your body and mind, what additives would create the most positive effect?

When we think about health from a microwins perspective, let's be inclusive. I include three subcategories under health: mouth, movement, and maker.

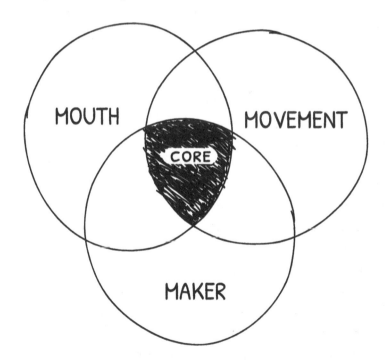

Mouth takes into account what I eat and drink. Am I consuming long-term, energy-producing foods? Am I avoiding processed foods? Am I staying hydrated? Can my body use what I put inside of it to help me run at an optimal level?

Movement centers on not just how much exercise I get but also where I exercise. How much time am I spending with my feet in dirt and grass? How much time is the sun hitting my body? Movement could encapsulate everything from weights to yoga, but context matters. Oftentimes, *where* we do the thing affects *how* we do the thing. This may seem counterintuitive, but rest and recovery are linchpins to movement. The absence of being in motion enables our body and spirit to recover. I think back to when I would beg my mother to not force me to take a nap, but in the summertime, I was forced to get one hour of sleep after lunch. Many times, I would feign sleep until the clock struck 1:30 p.m., then bolt up from the floor and head for the woods to play. Today, I incorporate a nap of at least 45 minutes into my daily regimen.

And finally, we come to maker. First things first: believe what you want to believe. I'm not here to judge you. We live in a nontolerant world that conflates what someone believes with who they are. I have spent enough time around humans to know that what they say they believe does not necessarily influence how they act. At this point in my life, I am focusing on spirituality over religion. This could involve reading scripture, meditation, prayer, and daily affirmations.

What I've found at the age of 45 is that I inhabit a body that is quite different from the one I had at 25. Those law school blackjack escapades would last until the wee hours of the morning. It wasn't uncommon for us to pull back into Cambridge at 5 a.m. I'd get three hours of sleep, and head to my 8:30 a.m. constitutional law class. I could sit through four classes, get an 8-mile run in through Cambridge, and not even think about napping.

Twenty years later, just typing that series of events makes me tired. In short, we are not who we once were. It's common to think of aging as a process that takes place over decades, when in fact, every single day our bodies undergo extreme upheaval. Nearly 330 billion cells turn over in our body every single day.[2] This churn takes place at the cellular level, obviously undetectable to our eyes and brain. Every morning that we awake, we are literally and figuratively a new creature. Reinvention is built into our genetic code.

The body keeps count and so should we. No, I don't mean we should obsess over the molecular implosions firing inside of our bodies, but we have to be vigilant observers of what our body is telling us. Soreness and fatigue are signals that something is off-kilter.

If you're anything like me, you cringe every time the check engine light goes off in your car. I am a chronic avoider. As soon as I see it light up my dashboard, I do a quick scan of the temp gauge to make sure the engine isn't running hot, and get on with my drive. Immediately my mind goes to worse-case scenarios. Then, I think of how I don't want to deal with those scenarios. And finally I keep driving down the road, making sure that I cannot see my dashboard in my peripheral vision.

When it comes to health, our bodies are just like the vehicles we drive. Sooner or later, warnings turn into repairs. But while you have time (and if you're reading this book, then you have time because you're still alive), don't belittle the impact of small changes. Merely adding a green smoothie to my daily routine created positive spillover effects. I couldn't look at my beloved Cherry Coke the same. It felt as if drinking a Coke would cancel the benefit of chugging the early morning smoothie. So, I gave up Cokes.

Whether we focus on mouth, movement, or maker, our future selves will thank us for the attention we pay to health today.

Deep Dive: How Small Can You Go?

Take the three following health categories and write one aspect for each that you would like to focus on with your microwins.

For example, let's take mouth. Perhaps you'd like to focus on eating fewer processed foods, drinking more water, or drinking less coffee.

Mouth

_____

_____

_____

_____

Movement

_____

_____

_____

Maker

_____

_____

_____

_____

Scan the following QR code to download microwins resources and join the movement.

SCAN CODE TO JOIN THE
MICROWINS MOVEMENT

WWW.MICROWINS.CO

11

The Microwins System

The Microwins System is simple. I have tried a litany of self-help hacks claiming to improve everything from time management to anxiety. For each of our domains (work, family, and health), I've read a library's worth of nonfiction books. Every book came with a system. And in all honesty, I can admit that I gave up on most of those systems because I wasn't seeing quick results.

I believe that most self-improvement systems work *if you do*. Put differently, systems work when people work. It's not enough to know what to do. Most people know what to do, but few people do what they know. The most well-developed plans are pointless without human execution.

Let's walk through the Microwins System. Don't worry; nothing you read in this section of the book will require you to do complex math. You won't have to maintain reams of records or an approach to crafting and executing the microwins that will shift your life for the better.

MOST PEOPLE KNOW WHAT TO DO, BUT FEW PEOPLE DO WHAT THEY KNOW.

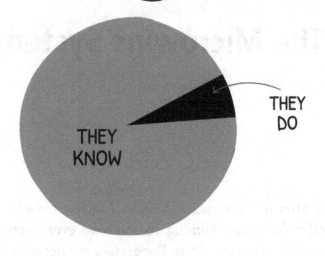

Step 1: Reimagine Yourself

I have a sneaky suspicion that most of us have given up on life. That is not to say that we don't want to live anymore. Rather, we have arrived at the conclusion there isn't more *life* left. We believe our best days are in the past and the window of opportunity for reinvention has closed.

I find myself slipping into this malaise sometimes. As I sit in bumper-to-bumper traffic, transporting my children between our home and their respective schools, I wonder, "Is this the way it all ends?"

Routine is the nemesis of reinvention.

Your imagination is the intellectual property that no one can replicate. Artificial intelligence can attempt to mimic it. But human imagination has no equal.

To reimagine your life, play the "What-If Game."

What if you moved to a different city?

What if you took those art classes at your local community college?

What if you asked to shadow your friend who owns a bakery?

Reimagining your life doesn't need to involve a eureka moment. In the chase for big breakthroughs, we tend to trivialize the tiny tweaks that can set us on a path of renewal. Instead of succumbing to life's inertia, embrace the two words that will jumpstart your new life: *what if.*

EMBRACE THE TWO WORDS THAT WILL JUMPSTART YOUR NEW LIFE

Step 2: Identify Three Macrowins

One thing I learned as a coach is that athletes play the game of football for a variety of reasons. Most fans assume that all NFL players have an insatiable love for the game. This seems reasonable, right? Why else would someone subject their bodies, safety, and future health to high-speed body collisions if they didn't love the work?

Well, do you love your job? Some of you are thinking, "Hell, yeah, I do, Daron! I can't get enough of selling commercial real estate or teaching kindergartners." Some of you are firmly in the "it's okay crowd." And still a few of you (if not more) are thinking, "Hell, no. I can't stand my job."

If all of you filled out a job satisfaction survey, the results would mirror a bell curve. A large group of "it's okay" people are surrounded by peers on the extremes. Well, the same holds true for the NFL. I coached guys who played the game because they were the biggest and fastest humans wherever they went. The game came easily to them. They played football because they were good at it, not because they truly loved the game. On one team, there was a defensive lineman whom I befriended. During down times at practice, we'd chat. Sometimes we'd talk before or after our defensive meetings. One day, he said something that nearly knocked me over, "You know, Coach, I don't really even like football." I turned to him in disbelief. One of the most dominating players in our division was telling me that he didn't love something that he had spent the majority of his life doing.

"The thing is, people don't see me as anything but a football player," he said. "I'm just doing this until I figure out what I really want to do."

As you think about your macrowins, I want you to take the three domains (work, family, and health) and zoom into a close look at what a better version of you looks like in each domain.

Take work, for example. You could choose to identify your day job or pick a side craft. Silence any limitations that others have placed on you and your capacity to excel. Make it personal. What would it look like to become the best writer that you could be? How would it feel to grow into a reliable leader on your team? The beautiful thing about macrowins is that you own them.

Step 3: Isolate Key Microwins

Now that you've identified your macrowins, it's time to isolate the microwins that will move you closer to realizing that BAWDY goal. Remember, this is not a 20-, 30-, or 60-day challenge. I know that "challenges" are all the rave, but we're not here for short-term gratification. We are building a practice and practice begins with chasing three microwins each day.

Let's say your macrowins are learn photography (work), strengthen your marriage (family), and run a 10K (health). We have a macrowin in each domain so we are ready to plot our daily work.

Our next step is to pick a small unit of victory that would feed into each macrowin. Here's what it could look like:

MACROWIN	MICROWIN
Learn photography.	Buy new camera.
Strengthen marriage.	Have date night with partner.
Run a 10K.	Walk for 20 minutes.

How does this look? Not too bad, eh? Well, remember that we are always trying to stack the deck in our favor. We search for ways to blunt any resistance on our completion of a microwin. So, let's ask ourselves, Can we go smaller? And the answer is, Of course! Take a look at what happens when we downsize:

MACROWIN	MICROWIN
Learn photography.	Look at specs for three new cameras.
Strengthen marriage.	Select options for date night with partner.
Run a 10K.	Walk for 10 minutes.

We relieve a lot of self-imposed pressure when we downsize our daily microwins. Our mission is to continuously shrink our microwins until we make it extremely difficult to miss the mark.

Step 4: Go!

I've noticed something about myself: the more I deliberate the less I deliver. With nine years of expensive higher education under my belt, I can quickly devolve into a mental game of cat and mouse. It sounds like this:

Well, first, I need to do this.
And then I need check in with so-and-so.
I should probably listen to that podcast episode.

Preparation has its place, but movement is life's best teacher. The solution to avoid the paralysis of overthinking and the recklessness of impulsiveness is the **PSA method: prep, schedule,** and **advance.**

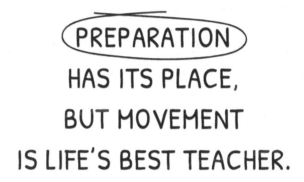

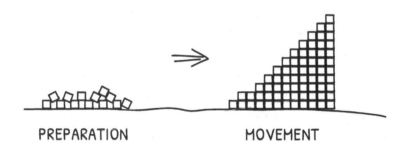

Prep

The best preparation for tomorrow's microwins takes place tonight. I live with six incredible humans, and I know that as soon as everyone wakes up, I lose control of some parts of my day. A child could leave her water bottle at home. A child could leave a permission slip at home. Soccer practice could get moved from 6:30 to 6:00 p.m. All three of these unforeseen occurrences happened in the last week alone.

It's important that you make room for microwins before you wake up. If you're trying to exercise more, place your workout clothes on the floor right beside your bed. Heck, I even sleep in my running shorts five nights out of the week. In the *Momentum* part of this book, you'll learn more about night routines, but let's just agree that 5 minutes of preparation tonight can eliminate 15 minutes of indecision tomorrow.

Schedule

If you're a digital calendar user, assign a color to your microwins. On my calendar microwins appear in yellow. If you're a tactile person and prefer paper calendars, use a colored pen to plan when and where you'll execute your microwins. Create no-fly zones (NFZs) around those blocks of time. I have NFZs plastered across my calendar and my wife and chief of staff know to never schedule anything that conflicts with them. Sure, there is the occasional emergency (or parent-teacher conference) that cannot be avoided. But these are rare occurrences because I treat my NFZs as sacred spaces. From the early morning writing sessions to the afternoon backyard composting sessions with my daughter to the late-night checkers game with my son, these micro-moments are who I am and represent the best of who I want to become. So, as you draw borders around your NFZs, understand that you're charting the boundaries of your most meaningful work.

Advance

This is the part of the story where I remind you to not overthink or trivialize your microwin. Go for it! Advance and move forward. Pick the easiest microwin for your daily list of three, and chase it as soon as you wake up. Frequently, I list drinking a green smoothie or running three miles as one of my health microwins. As soon as my alarm goes off, I'm on a mission to get that microwin checked off my list. And when you finish, check it off your list. That's right. Take out your pen and check it off of your list as soon as you complete it. Nothing compares to the feeling of notching a victory before lunchtime.

Step 5: Give Yourself Some Grace (and Then Get Back Up Again)

It is going to be tempting to get down on yourself on days that you complete one (or none) of your three microwins. I've been there. A tactical mistake would be to view each day's microwins as a zero-sum game. Taking this approach will only set you up for failure, because you'll likely shelve the system as soon as you collect a couple of subpar productions.

Don't confuse a game with the season. Sometimes, being on the ground level of our own lives blinds us with a granular view of our progress. Instead of comparing yourself against a perfect performance, make fewer judgments and ask more questions:

> *What can I alter about the people, places, and things around me in order to put myself in a better position to nab those microwins?*
> *How can I alter the timing of when I tackle my microwins?*
> *Should I recruit a partner to increase my accountability to the system?*

A defeatist default approach would be to throw up your hands and say, "To hell with this system, it's not going to work for me." But remember: you deserve better from you.

In the last section of this book, I identify the main culprits of self-sabotage and provide you with the 17 Laws of Momentum to keep you engaged in this quest to conquer your macrowins. But first, let's do one last deep dive.

Deep Dive: How Low Can You Go?

Let's practice converting macrowins into microwins. First, write your three macrowins here. Then, convert them into microwins. Now here's the kicker: *do it again*. Shrink that microwin down into a smaller unit of victory. Feel free to reference the previous example to guide you work.

Work macrowin: _____

Family macrowin: _____

Health macrowin: _____

Round 1:

Macrowin 1: _____	Microwin 1: _____
Macrowin 2: _____	Microwin 2: _____
Macrowin 3: _____	Microwin 3: _____

Round 2:

Microwin 1: _____	Microwin 1A: _____
Microwin 2: _____	Microwin 2A: _____
Microwin 3: _____	Microwin 3A: _____

Scan the following QR code to download microwins resources and join the movement.

SCAN CODE TO JOIN THE
MICROWINS MOVEMENT

WWW.MICROWINS.CO

PART

III

Momentum

The older I get the better I understand something that my junior high track coach told me: "Coming out of the blocks fast is great. Just remember: The finish is more important than the start." In *Momentum*, I share 17 laws that will help you sustain forward progress. Oh, and make sure you don't skip Law 17 to find out how you finish.

Here are a few of the laws in Chapter 12:

Law 3: Swallow the Minnow

Yep, you read that right. Take that minnow like a tequila shot. In this law, you'll find out what the minnow is and why you should take it down as soon as you can.

Law 10: Move First, Deliberate Later

We had a saying in the NFL: Stiff hips sink ships. If you can't or won't move, you're not just a liability to your team; you're an impediment to yourself.

Law 14: Aim for 10 Minutes Instead of 10,000 Hours

Ten thousand may be the most popular number in the self-help world. With the Microwins System, we focus on momentum not mastery.

CHAPTER

12

The 17 Laws
of Momentum

Flip back to Chapter 6. Go to the deep dive and read your macrowins aloud (if you haven't crafted your macrowins, then do it now). What did you hear? I'm not just talking about the particular words. But how did it sound to read your macrowins back to yourself? Hopefully, you could feel your body respond to the words coming out of your mouth. Was there any tingle in the belly? Any quivering in your voice? Did the back of your neck get involved?

Law 1: Marry Your Macrowins

IT DOESN'T MATTER
<u>WHEN</u> YOU START,
WHAT MATTERS IS THAT
YOU START.

This existence is riddled with responsibilities. "Obligations" will overthrow an existence if you allow them to. Macrowins, however, is where we take our stand. It's the wide open territory where we plant our flag and stake our claim. I have worked with hundreds of people who've used the Microwins System simply because they saw the daily pictures that I would post to social media of my 4×6 index cards. I watched them race out of the gates as if they were running the 100-meter dash in the Olympics. For the first few days, every microwins-related post featured them going 3-for-3.

And then cracks started to emerge. One day they'd go for 2-for-3, the next day 1-for-3, and before long, they stopped posting at all. Let me be clear: you don't *have to* share your microwins with the world. This is a personal process. Although I regularly post my microwins on social media (#Microwins), there are times when the content is sensitive (to me or the people I love) and so I don't.

People lose momentum for a variety of reasons but a common pitfall is racing out of the blocks before committing to the race. Remember in high school when you had that friend who played a certain sport just because she could? She neither loved nor hated volleyball; she just played because it's something she had always done.

Well, you need to be in love with your macrowins if you hope to have any chance of making progress with your microwins. Strain your macrowins through the BAWDY test that we discussed in Chapter 6. Here's a refresher: BAWDY stands for: (1) bright, (2) aspirational, (3) worth it, (4) delusional, and (5) why not?

All five of the features are important but the third one becomes pivotal as you're trudging through the highs and lows of the system. Somewhere in your past, you set a historical precedent for achieving the unexpected. There's a peak that you can point to (and I don't have to know you in order to write this statement with confidence), on which you defied the doubters around you and even your own expectations.

Just because some years might separate you from that moment doesn't mean that you can't marshal the same resilience to do it again. But *you* have to believe. As I was typing those cover letters in my overpriced and undersized apartment in Cambridge, I believed that I would land in the NFL. That macrowin—to become an NFL head coach— was BAWDY enough to keep me up at night.

I slept with spreadsheets on my mind. *Maybe I should send another letter to Coach Kubiak. Tomorrow, I'll call the number for the Chargers and see if they received my cover letter.*

How far is Foxborough from here? Maybe I can just drive over and hang out in the coaches' parking lot and see if I can catch Belichick or one of the assistants. My head overflowed with delusional thoughts, and I converted each one of them into microwins.

I wrote follow-up letters to Coach Kubiak with the Houston Texans.

No response.

I called the Chargers to see if they received my cover letter and the woman who picked up the phone told me that they probably did but they received hundreds of letters every week.

I sat outside the Patriots' stadium in Foxborough. A security officer told me to leave or he would escort me to the exit. I left.

I did everything I could possibly think of in order to break into the coaching fraternity. Why? Because I made a vow to my macrowin. And this level of deranged commitment to a goal is what will keep you in the race.

Law 2: Evolve Away

WARNING: Law 2 may appear to contradict Law 1. Trust me, they can coexist.

In August 2022, Serena Williams announced that she was "evolving away" from tennis. A *Vogue* piece, "Serena Williams Says Farewell to Tennis on Her Own Terms— And in Her Own Words," captures the sport's most decorated player. In it, she wrote, "Maybe the best word to describe what I'm up to is evolution. I'm here to tell you that I'm evolving away from tennis, toward other things that are important to me. A few years ago I quietly started Serena Ventures, a venture capital firm. Soon after that, I started a family. I want to grow that family.[1]

Evolving away. In our world, the language about transition is fraught with negative connotations. Quitting, resigning, retiring, walking away. All of these terms are met with reactions that range from celebration to derision. What Serena does so elegantly in this open letter is reframe the moment. She understands that for many commentators and sports enthusiasts, nothing will shake their belief that she is giving up on the game of tennis. But the tone and tilt of her writing isn't meant for them. Her words reek of vulnerability. Although she understood that the pull quotes from the text would land on ESPN and books like this one, it is clear that she is writing for herself. She's doing this for Serena.

From our earliest days in grade school, American children learn about the American Revolution. I can still see a picture of George Washington standing in a boat as it lurches through the icy Delaware. Growing up in Texas, I learned as much (if not more) Texas history as I did American history. At least I learned my teachers' version of it. I can't tell you how many times I heard the story of the Alamo.

The American ethos centers on revolution. This fierce independence and relentless fight for autonomy. I believe sometimes we look at our personal lives and believe that unless we stage an all-out revolution, we lack any chance to reinvent ourselves and revamp our lives.

Enter evolution. "I'm here to tell you that I'm evolving away from tennis, toward other things that are important to me," Serena writes. Don't feel guilty or reluctant to evolve away from the things that once gave you joy. The things that were important to you in a previous life. Today's version of you is a *new you*. Embrace that person.

The chains that weld us to the past are welded by expectations of the people around us. When I shunned the law for football, I imagined the disappointment of my former teachers. Mind you, I had not seen some of them since the day I graduated from high school. Years had passed since I'd heard their voice. Yet, I imagined the disapproval of a decision that I was making hundreds of miles away from my hometown. A player I coached on the Browns retired from football in 2019. He and I had a chance to grab coffee in Austin as he was in the city for the annual South by Southwest. A steady buildup of minor injuries had reached a tipping point. He had problems mustering the physical strength to get out of bed every morning. He had been ready to "evolve away" from the game of football for nearly five years, but the one thing that held him back was his fear of how his extended family would see him. Would they view him as a quitter? Would he attract the same awe and respect as he had when he donned NFL jerseys? "It wasn't my pride, Coach, it was my ego," he said. After leaving the game, his circle shrunk but his corner grew stronger.

If you are considering a life shift (and by virtue of buying this book, I can assume that you are), please understand that nothing you choose will pacify all of the people around you. So, don't even try. Embrace evolution as a natural progression in your journey on this planet.

Law 3: Swallow the Minnow

SWALLOW THE MINNOW.

Allegedly, it was Mark Twain who said (or wrote), "Eat a live frog first thing in the morning and nothing worse will happen to you the rest of the day." As with most attributions to the 19th-century writer, no one can point to any verifiable evidence that he ever uttered the words. Notwithstanding, Brian Tracy built an entire book on the concept in *Eat That Frog! 21 Great Ways to Stop Procrastinating and Get More Done in Less Time*. He argued that, when faced with two seemingly equal tasks of importance, take on the more important task first.

Tracy writes, "You cannot eat every tadpole and frog in the pond, but you can eat the biggest and ugliest one, and that will be enough, at least for the time being. If you have to eat two frogs, eat the ugliest one first."[2]

I propose a different approach: *swallow the minnow*.

I am what you may call a morning person. I crave the quiet and calm of predawn hours. Before anyone else wakes up, I can indulge in the work that is most important to me. As soon as my alarm goes off, I grasp for the lowest hanging fruit on my list of microwins. I approach the mornings as a sprinter, I want to build as much forward momentum as I can as early as I can. I know that planting this flag of early success into my day will become a reference point. During the dips of the day when I lack motivation (typically before and after lunch), I'll point back to the morning and say, "Wait, I can do this. Let's go, Daron."

So, when I wake up, I look for the smallest, slowest-moving minnow swimming in my fish bowl of microwins. And once I find it, I grab the little critter and shoot it like tequila. My goal is to build momentum to sustain my work throughout the day. This means that I place less focus on the relative size of the microwin and pay more attention to the probability that I can get it done *now*.

This is a form of stacking the deck. We want to create ideal environments for us to win as many of our microwins as possible. For example, my health microwins typically involve drinking a green smoothie. Green smoothies are exactly what they sound like, smoothies dominated by green things and very low in sugar. Kale, broccoli, and bok choy are a few examples of ingredients that find their way into my blender on a daily basis.

You know what I realized when I first started drinking green smoothies? Because I didn't use sugar (no sugary fruits or artificial additives), the smoothies didn't taste that good. In fact, a lot of my concoctions taste like blended grass.

But, the feeling that I got after downing 32 ounces of grass was astronomical. Call it a placebo effect or the power of kale, but I would be motivated to begin my workout as soon as I swallowed the last drop of green smoothie. I point to the motivational buildup that comes with notching early victories. The reluctant brain that would rather be lying in bed or scrolling through TikTok says, "Okay, I guess this woman is ready to attack the day, so let's help her."

So, when you're deciding which microwin to pursue, do the one that is the easiest to check off. We tend to think of progress in terms of weeks, months, or days. But games are won in the trenches. Each play turns into a series that builds into possessions. Those possessions turn into halves. Halves turn into games.

Those seemingly unnoticeable plays influence the final score. Get points on the board early by pursuing the lowest hanging fruit. And this brings me to night routines.

Law 4: Revamp Your Night Routines

In Law 2, we talked about why you should look for the smallest microwin swimming inside of your fishbowl of life, reach down, and swallow it without thinking twice. Well, let's revamp a period of your daily prep that will make that daily minnow pill a tad bit easier.

Have you noticed how people have fallen in love with "morning rituals"? It seems like every self-help publication and guru has some top five list of how to approach your mornings.

Frictionless mornings, however, are by-products of methodical nights. As someone who enjoys the serenity of the early mornings, I recognize how 30 minutes of preparation every night can save me an hour of scrambling in the morning. Here are my top five night routines to inject more space and time for you to experience a successful launch to your day.

First, pick out your clothes. One of the most annoying aspects of my childhood was ironing my clothes on Sunday afternoon. My mom was a stickler for this practice. I hated it. I would always think (but never say to mom), "Why can't I just wait and iron my clothes in the morning?" Not only would I have to iron them on Sundays, but I would also have to set each day's attire out before going to bed.

Today, picking my clothes every night is a staple of my internal systems. Former president Barack Obama told author Michael Lewis in a 2012 interview, "You'll see I wear only gray or blue suits. I'm trying to pare down decisions. I don't want to make decisions about what I'm eating or wearing. Because I have too many other decisions to make."[3] The fewer mental computing chips that you spend on deciding between black or brown, the more cognitive horsepower you have for higher level tasks—like executing your microwins.

Second, let's focus on the kitchen. Coffee. Oatmeal. Smoothies. Lunches for the next day. Take your most time-consuming morning kitchen routines and push them back to the previous night. My preference is to prepare my breakfast (oatmeal, a green smoothie, and scrambled eggs) right after I finish eating dinner. If you're a coffee drinker, open your coffeemaker, throw in a filter, fill filter with coffee and pour water the evening before. If you eat cereal, take out your bowl and spoon and place it where you eat. These micro movements add up.

Before I come to my third tip, let me pose a question: have you ever heard of email bankruptcy? It's a practice in which you delete all of the emails in your inbox and start from scratch. My third night routine is much simpler: succinctly answer the three most pressing emails in your inbox. These three emails are likely to take up more mental real estate than we can afford. Answer them and then . . . close every window in your browser.

That's our fourth strategy and you read it right: close every single window in your browser. All of them. There is one exception. If one of your microwins for the following day requires you to use your computer, then leave one tab open with the necessary site. For example, as I am writing this book, I save all of the chapters to a Google Drive folder, which then gets shared to editors. Because all of my "work" microwins involve writing this book, the file with the corresponding file that I will be working on each day is the only tab that stays permanently open and it is the only tab I see when I open my computer at 5 a.m.

A frictionless morning is the breakfast of champions. Practice the discipline to follow your night routines and prepare for takeoff!

Law 5: Keep Past Wins in Your Hip Pocket

I carry two copies of my first book, *Call an Audible*, with me wherever I go. I'm sure to some of you this seems a little vain, but let me explain how carrying those two books help me to keep going.

We've talked about how our past peaks and pits influence our perception of what's possible in the future. I'm just like you. During moments of despair, I can feel my body slowly oozing into the pits of my life. Like water, our mindsets will take the path of least resistance and settle there. It's dark down there, and light has difficulty traveling to its depths. I liken my books to flashlights.

One of the copies is for me to gift to someone. I've given the book to fellow passengers on a Southwest flight, Lyft drivers, and the crossing guard at my kids' school. The second book, however, is something I will never give away. The other copy is what I call a "peak ____." This copy is tattered. The binder is coming loose. A few pages are missing. A few times a day (and at my lowest points even more) I take this copy out of my backpack and just look at it. I read the cover. I say my name aloud. "I did this," I tell myself in an audible voice; "I wrote this book, and I will write another one."

My cellphone wallpaper is another constant reminder of my past success. If you could have watched me play football as a freshman in high school, you wouldn't have been impressed. I was undersized with average speed and below-average awareness. In short, I wasn't that good, but I loved playing the game. The camaraderie of the locker room, the scent of freshly cut grass in the fall, and the goal of cracking the starting lineup by the time I reached my senior year kept me motivated to get better. I loaded up on protein shakes. I maxed out on peanut butter and banana sandwiches. I ran up and down the blacktop road that bordered our home. I lifted weights during the summer. And by the time I reached my senior year, I made the starting lineup.

To cap off the season, I was selected as the 1st-Team All-District strong safety. When I look back on my life, I am more proud of that achievement than anything else that I accomplished because I can still remember where I started. I can still feel the shame of being on the sideline as a freshman, embarrassed because my mom and dad were watching their son ride the bench.

Regardless of where you are in life today, there are past victories that you must revisit. Don't trivialize them. Perhaps it was a junior high production in which you played a key role, or maybe it was a college chemistry exam that you scored a B. We have a tendency to inflate the successes of others while minimizing our own.

As we fight to create and sustain momentum on our microwins, take those peak moments from the past and place them front and center into the Microwins System. These artifacts arc visual reminders not just of who we once were but also what we are capable of.

Law 6: Heed the Law of Extraction

A few years back, I was in Oakland for a keynote, and with some spare time on my hands I decided to visit a local plant shop. As you've probably gathered by some of my gardening references in this book, I am an ardent gardener. I've even considered installing cameras in my garden so I can keep up with my plants' progress while I'm away.

As I walked into this plant shop, I casually noticed a sign at the entrance, *"Please take responsibility for the energy that you bring into this space."* I walked right by the sign and then stopped in my tracks. I took a deep breath. Walking backwards, I slowly mouthed the words on the sign again, *Please take responsibility for the energy that you bring into this space.*

Just thinking about the words and underlying message caused me to reflect on my day. My flight into SFO was late. A flight attendant forced me to gate-check my carry-on, even though I knew the overhead compartments were not full. A woman next to me spilled Coke in my lap. Yes, it had been one of those kinds of days. I had followed the plant shop online during the pandemic and figured a shot of chlorophyll would brighten my day.

I was looking for an external fix to an internal issue. This thought process animates our entire health care industry. Here's my problem; prescribe some pills or inject with some liquids to make them disappear. But as I thought about my mood, I wondered, "Am *I* the problem?" Sure, some things happened to me that I hadn't accounted for when I departed Austin that morning. But had any of the events caused catastrophic harm? No. Would I be able to recover from the mishaps. Of course. But it would require me to get intentional.

If you were to track down any one of my former players and ask him, "What is one of Coach Roberts's mantras?"

I guarantee his response would be, "Control the controllables." It's something that I said at least once every day. In a sport that receives so much attention and media scrutiny, I would always stress the need for my guys to control what they could control: effort, attitude, and energy.

Energy is a game of nouns.

The following morning, I delivered my keynote and a woman waited to meet me. Before I could say, "Hello" she started ranting to me about her hotel room's temperature (Note: I just met the woman and lacked any authority [or desire] to adjust her room temp.) I just nodded and waited for her to finish.

> Me: *I hope you'll excuse me. It was so nice to meet you.*

And just like that, I walked away. To be honest, it was awkward, but the sense of relief outweighed the social tension. I'm sure many of you may be thinking, *That was rude*. But, I've learned that negativity carries an electric charge. If you linger in its vicinity, it will alter you. An appraisal of your relationships will confirm this point. Have you ever spent some time with friends, perhaps a coffee meetup or brunch, and walked away feeling drained? A meeting that should have been life-giving turned into an exercise in depletion.

On my plane ride back to Austin, a man sat on my row and immediately started complaining about his Uber driver. Thank God it was a Southwest flight. I immediately got up and moved two rows back. Extraction.

In short, take responsibility for both the energy that you carry and the energy that you surround yourself with. You own the exclusive right to exit energy-depleting environments. Exercise it.

Law 7: Keep Positive People in Close Proximity

Proximity. The word derives from the Latin term "proximus," which translates into *nearest*. When was the last time you took an inventory of your nearest relationships? I am talking about an honest methodical accounting of the people in your life. It is easy to complain right after a negative episode with someone. "She's always _____," or "Every time I talk to him, he brings up _____," but we tend to make quick assessments of a person's character or personality—we don't adjust our orientation. Previously in the book, we stressed the importance of noticing what lights you up. Well, when it comes to momentum, it is time to notice *who lights us up.*

When I was growing up, like most adolescents, I yearned to be cool. Junior high is a malleable time for a kid. It's the first time that I recognized that there was a social hierarchy forming within the people in my school. The cafeteria and playground turned into a clustering experiment. You were expected to find "your people" and stick with them.

My dad noticed that I was gravitating toward the groups that I thought would give me the most clout. "Show me your friends, and I'll show you your future," he'd say whenever I'd recount an episode from school that featured unsavory behavior. His words didn't land with me until I got to college. In college, it became clear to me that social circles were operating systems. The food I ate. The movies I watched. The music I listened to. The aspirations I formed. All of these things were heavily influenced by the people around me.

In many ways, none of us ever left junior high. We still find ourselves deeply influenced by the people around us and to a certain extent, we are affected by the people who are around the people who are around us. Yes, you read that correctly. It's not just the people in your immediate circle who shape what you think, how you feel, and what you do. No, there is a spillover effect between overlapping circles. One study illustrates this cascade effect. A team of researchers looked at data that had been collected for the Framingham Heart Study. The study assessed 12,067 people between 1971 to 2003. The researchers found that "a person's chances of becoming obese increased by 57% . . . if he or she had a friend who became obese in a given interval." Moreover, if that friend had a friend who was obese, the impact to you would be a 20% increase in the chances that you would become obese. This data combined with other findings led the team to conclude that "network phenomena appear to be relevant to the biologic and behavioral trait of obesity, and obesity appears to spread through social ties."[4]

Now, let me be clear. The analyses focused on obesity. Yet, I think we can attest to the presence of this cascade effect through our interactions with the people around us.

I'll give you one example. How many times has a friend mentioned that she is starting a new diet or "challenge"?

Before you know it, you're doing the challenge right alongside them. You're eating quinoa and taking shots of carrot juice without hesitation. This is the power of proximity. Our people and our people's people influence our behavior.

Michael Housman and Dylan Minor conducted a study of more than 2,000 employees of a large technology firm.[5] They dove into two years' worth of data to analyze the proximal effects of workplace placement. Put differently, how much does one's spatial and working relationship to someone else affect outcomes such as productivity, effectiveness, and quality? What the researchers found supports the case for being diligent with our personal and professional associations. Another study found that "if toxic employees were near each other, it increased the probability that one of them would be terminated by 27%. But in contrast to productivity and quality spillover, any type of worker seemed susceptible to toxic spillover. If a toxic worker sat next to a nontoxic worker, the toxic worker's influence won out, and the nontoxic worker had an increased chance of becoming toxic."[6]

This may seem like common sense: beware of surrounding yourself with toxic people. Common sense, however, is not common practice. Sometimes we accommodate the company of toxic individuals because of our adjacent relationships. Because we are friends with Jerome and Taj is a friend of Jerome, I must also be a friend of Taj. This logic rings hollow. You are responsible for *guarding* your energy, and that means that you have to comb through the guest list of your life with the precision of a wedding planner crafting a seating chart.

Proximity fuels propensity. As you travel the road through microwins, stay close to the people who exude positive attitudes and behaviors. Trust your gut. My grandmother would put it this way, "Once people show you who they are, *believe them.*"

Law 8: Learn a New Language

In Principle 4, we learned the power of wiretapping your mental chatter. We have a reflexive tendency to respond to adversity with the language of submission. As a challenge looms on the horizon, not only does our physiology change but also our language follows the body's lead.

How would our perspective change if we learned a new language? No, I'm not going to ask you to download Duolingo or any other language app and pick up a new tongue. Rather, let's spend some time explicating common words and phrases that we use during periods of disenchantment and despair. Notice how a slight language shift changes the attitudinal directions in two examples.

But → And

Both *but* and *and* are conjunctions. They serve as a bridge between two or more ideas. You may notice that as our mood spirals downward, *but* becomes more prevalent in our speech.

"I would really like to do A, *but* I don't have enough time."

"Things were going well with my microwins, *but* then X happened."

But leaves little room for rebuttal. It makes a definitive thud in our language, as if to say, "Well, that's the end of that!" The word *and*, however, creates space for opportunity. Look at a couple of examples.

"I would really like to do A, *and* in order to make time, I am going to do B, C, and D."

"Things were going well with my microwins until X happened, *and* to get back on track, I am going to do B, C, and D."

Here's what I find when I jump through the mental calisthenics of shifting *but* to *and*: I am more intentional. I take the time to really evaluate the validity of my excuses. Did I go dark on my microwins because of an incident that happened *or* because of my poor response to the thing that happened? The overwhelming majority of derailments in my life are by-products of my willingness to confront the root cause of the problem.

And is a term of ownership.

Hard → Challenging

We are going through a parenting phase in which our children are meeting new subjects in school like algebra, biology, and calculus. A common refrain that can be heard at our dining room table in the evenings is "This is hard!"

A few years ago, we experimented with a language shift. We replaced *hard* with *challenging*. My wife and I were vigilant. Every time we heard someone utter the word *hard*, we'd chime in with "You mean *challenging*." Over the course of a year, we would hear our children tell their siblings, "Not *hard* just *challenging*."

My wife and I have yet to figure out this parenting game. I'm not sure we will ever get it right, and I'm not even sure what "getting it right" means. But there are these minor mentality shifts that signal we may be on the right track. In fact, after noticing that I also gravitated toward the word *hard*, I started monitoring my own language. I made small changes, and I continue to notice the words that I use and the effect they have on my body.

Try it. Take an inventory of the words that you use. Do they light or dim your journey?

Law 9: Shun Perfection, Chase Consistency

SHUN PERFECTION,
CHASE CONSISTENCY.

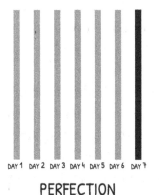

PERFECTION

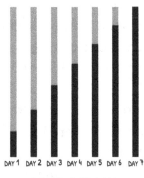

CONSISTENCY

During the 2023–2024 NBA season, Shai Gilgeous-Alexander broke Kevin Durant's Oklahoma Thunder record for games scoring 30 points or more in a season. After posting his 47th 30-point performance of the season, Gilgeous-Alexander put up an incredible stat line: he scored 37 points and added five rebounds and six assists.

"My whole life is consistent. Everything I do, from what I eat to when I sleep to my recovery to my loved ones, everything's consistent. And it's a routine for me at this point."[7]

My whole life is consistent. Gilgeous-Alexander is an elite basketball player. Although I watched basketball as a kid, my first love was baseball. There was only one problem—I wasn't a good baseball player, and I knew it. My coaches knew it. My parents knew it. But for a five-year stretch, I kept showing up for tryouts in our citywide baseball league. I was good enough to make a team. I could play great defense. I could even pitch a little. But my Achilles heel was hitting. I practiced and practiced and practiced. My dad nailed an old tire to the side of a live oak tree that grew in our backyard. As soon as the school bus deposited me at the end of our driveway, I would run into my house, inhale a snack, and grab my bat. For hours, I would work on my swing. Eye placement. Toe placement. Chin placement. I isolated every aspect of a swing, and tried to get as close as I could to replicating the swing of my childhood hero—Ken Griffey Jr.

In the 1980s, recording anything—whether it be on the television or radio—was a major feat. I convinced my dad to create a rig where I could record Seattle Mariners games on VHS. I then took those games, and spliced Griffey's into slices. I would watch the clips over and over and over again, until my parents practically forced me to go to bed.

I don't have the stats from my years playing on the Little League circuit, but I do have a stat that you might find surprising. At the time of writing this book, there are 303 members of Major League's Baseball Hall of Fame. I've visited the respective halls of fame of the three major sports: football, basketball, and baseball. Canton, Ohio. Springfield, Massachusetts. Cooperstown, New York. Nothing quite compares to Cooperstown. There's a rustic aspect to baseball's history in America that makes its history that much more special.

According to Baseball Reference, an online database of baseball statistics, the average batting average of MLB Hall of Famers is .303.[8] That translates into Hall of Famers getting a hit one out of every three times they go to the plate. One out of three. That's less than half. Put differently, for every 10 at-bats, this heralded group collectively failed to reach base 7 out of 10 times.

There are few professions in which missing the mark 7 out of 10 times, would be considered an achievement. But in the game of baseball, batting .300 is good. Why? Because the people who play the game have tacitly agreed on the standard.

As you approach your microwins on a daily basis, it will be tempting to want to go 3-for-3. For the past decade, I've kept banker's boxes indexed by year. In each folder, lies my daily microwins. Most of them are written on unlined 4×6 index cards. Others are on Starbucks cookie wrappers, Southwest Airlines napkins, and hotel stationery. There are days when I went 3-for-3. My microwins in work, family, and health all have a red check beside them. Conversely, there are days when I went 0-for-3. In a span of 24 hours, I couldn't eke out a single microwin.

Don't fall into the perfection trap. Perfection is the enemy of consistency. Perfection tends to lull us into a false belief in our capabilities. We start believing that there is something about us, some genetic trait or predisposition that makes us special. Nothing rivals the fall of human drunk with their own success. Daily progress, the building blocks of consistency, is a more reliable trait. Just missing the mark can be a beneficial outcome because it forces us to circle back on our practices. Where can we improve? What parts of the process could we tweak to get better?

This evolution is the mark of consistency. Forget about style points and stay the course.

Law 10: Move First, Deliberate Later

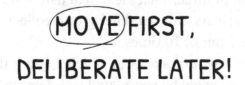

Some of my fondest memories from childhood revolve around the game of dominoes. I have a large extended family with more than 50 first cousins. During our annual family reunions, my uncles would sit around small tables and play round after round of dominoes.

If a player was taking his time before making a play, an opposing player would say, "Study long, study wrong." You can imagine what he meant. The more you tried to estimate the perfect play, the more likely it was that you were going to make a bad one.

Sayings like "Study long, study wrong" and "paralysis by analysis" touch on a sticking point for most of us who want to improve our lot: how do we determine the most optimal move?

There's a simple answer: we can't. Without the ability to fast-forward into the future, view the result of a decision, and then rewind back into the present, we can never be completely confident that the move we're going to make is the right one. Moreover, what do we really mean by "right"? If we're honest, we're usually referring to the decision that led to the least amount of loss and highest output of gains.

But take your life as a case study and think back to the peaks and pits of your existence. I am sure that you can trace some of your pits to a single decision that created a very discrete outcome. Conversely, some of your pits (and I'm sure some of your peaks as well) were preceded by decisions that, at the time, you were unaware would lead to the result.

In the 1950s, the physicist Hugh Everett proposed the "many-worlds interpretation" of quantum mechanics.[9] Everett presented a scenario in which you have a particle like an electron. According to Everett's interpretation, when we observe this electron, instead of the universe "deciding" on one outcome, it actually splits into multiple branches. In one branch, the electron is in one state, and in another branch, it's in a different state. Everett proposed that this branching occurs in an infinite loop, for every possible outcome of every quantum event.

His ideas gave birth to the notion of the "multiverse," where all possible realities are playing out across a spectrum of universes. Unfortunately, we don't have the luxury of operating in parallel universes (or maybe we do and just haven't figured out how to do so). We live in a world landlocked by our observations. We act, observe, interpret, and act again. At present, we don't wield the power to choose outcomes; rather, we move toward our intended goals and hope for the best.

Our agency lies in our power to move. A linebacker coach whom I worked with preached the same sermon to his players every day during practice, "See. Move. Adjust." See. Move. Adjust. No amount of research and deliberation can insulate us from the uncertainty that comes with life. Fret not; you always have the power to adjust.

Law 11: Travel the Road Until the Territory Speaks

For part of the writing of this book, I traveled to the Smoky Mountains. In short, the environment is perfect for continuous uninterrupted periods of reading, writing, and reflection. In October 2023, I had a chance to visit the Smokies for the first time as a participant in the Tremont Writers Conference. To call that week in the Smokies a perspective-changing experience would be an understatement. My family and I live in the city limits of one of the fastest-growing cities in America. Trains choo-choo and cars honk with reckless abandon. I am a sensitive sleeper. Every night, right after I release the blackout shades in our bedroom, I ask Alexa to pipe in pink noise.

The first thing that struck me during my stay in the Smokies was the absence of unnatural light and sound. The properties in the park lacked streetlights. I thought my cellphone flashlight would provide ample light to navigate the night. I was wrong. After a night of nearly breaking my hips trying to travel between two buildings, I relented. On the second day, I descended the mountains, pulled into a Dollar General, and bought a flashlight.

To get to the Smokies, I flew from Austin (through) Dallas into Knoxville. Then I rented a car, and made the 30-mile drive to Townsend. Using Google Maps, I wound my way through the Smokies, deliberately driving as slow as legally possible so I wouldn't find myself in a gutter. Google was telling me that I should exit onto a particular highway, but when I looked up, I could see construction vehicles lining the road and a man holding a sign pointing in the opposite direction from my Google guidance. The road was closed. After a two-mile detour, I landed back on the original route, but it was clear that the Google satellites weren't privy to the information that I had on the ground.

In the early 1930s the mathematician Alfred Korzybski formulated the idea that "the map is not the territory." Korzybski's primary objective was to illustrate the difference between our subjective perceptions and objective reality. Our "perceptions" could be understood as the map and the "objective reality" would translate into the territory. In short, what we think and even what we *think* we think differ from what actually exists.

So, how does this relate to microwins? Well, as we begin to plod away on our daily microwins, you will inevitably find that your notion of what could be possible and what is possible are two different things. I'll give you an example. To engender a closer relationship with my eldest son, I created microwins of playing two games of basketball with him after school. For an entire week, I couldn't make any progress. It was during late autumn, and I found that I was getting home after the sun set. Austin was unseasonably cold for that time of year and my wife wasn't too keen on me playing basketball with her son on a dimly lit court. "If he gets sick, that's on you," she said.

Then, I decided to shift the target. I wrote, "Help my son finish his homework." Every day, I walked into the house, placed my bag by the front door and sat at the kitchen table.

Me: *What you workin' on?*

Him: *Math; it's killing me.*

Me: *Mind if I take a look? It's been a while, but I may remember something about fractions.*

As it turns out, he didn't even want to play basketball. He appreciated my fumbling through Please Excuse My Dear Aunt Sally (the mnemonic device used to remember order of operations in mathematics) more than any jump shot I could have pulled off in the backyard.

Sometimes what we think we will see is very different than what we find. Instead of getting frustrated that your calculation was a bit off, assess, adapt, and advance.

Law 12: Recruit Your Roommates

"Daddy, are you ready to play dominoes?"

Jack's tenor signaled a recognition that he was fully aware that the microwins in my family domain was to play a game of dominoes with him before bedtime. We had just finished dinner, and I was sitting on the couch rereading one of my favorite books, *The War of Art* by Steven Pressfield. I placed a bookmark on the page and walked to the kitchen table.

"Your microwin for the day is to play a game of dominoes with me and my microwin," pointing to his chest for emphasis, "for the day is to beat you," he said. "So, let's both get our microwin done!"

I couldn't help but laugh. I took a seat, and proceeded to lose not one, but two games of dominoes to an eight-year-old.

How did Jack know that playing dominoes was a microwin for me? Well, I told him. When I first started the practice, I knew that I needed peer pressure. Sometimes, knowing that someone expects something of me, is looking forward to me doing something, is enough to make me do it. I call it positive peer pressure (PPP). PPP creates a healthy nudge in your daily microwins.

Every evening, I write down my microwins for the following day in a few places. First, I write them on an index card. Throughout the day, that index card goes everywhere I go. While I'm sitting in traffic or waiting in line at Starbucks, I take out the card and reread them. The list is always short and discrete so I can easily remember every word, but I find the act of rereading them keeps me centered. Like the play sheet that some quarterback's wear below their wrist, the microwins are my cheat sheet of go-to plays.

Second, I write them on my bathroom mirror with a bright red dry erase marker. While I'm brushing my teeth, braiding my daughter's hair, or shaving, I take a quick glance.

Finally, I write them on two wipe boards, one in the playroom of my house and the other in my garage. Over breakfast or during a snack, my children will ask about them. My wife sends text checkups throughout the day to encourage me. Moreover, I've witnessed a spillover effect. My eldest son has daily microwins for the number of basketball shots he will take. My youngest daughter has daily microwins for her after-school time in our garden. And my wife uses the system to guide her the way she spends her personal time.

I understand that everyone has a unique living situation. Perhaps you live alone. The visual reminders will help you stay on track. Or maybe you're surrounded by other humans. Try leaving breadcrumbs of microwins around your home and watch how your people respond. Microwins work well when pursued alone and even better with the people we love. Share the system with the people in your corner and watch them find ways to support your journey on the path to consistency. Go public in your home.

Law 13: Practice Cell Shabbat

In 2014, I met a witty, young undergraduate at the University of Texas, Jori Epstein. I had just spoken to her brother's graduating class, and Jori walks up to me and says, "Here's what I think worked in your speech, but here are a few things you should think about changing." After providing her unasked-for advice, I said, "Let's stay in contact. You're a rare one." And we did.

She was also attending UT and as she neared graduation a couple of years later, we met for lunch to discuss her thesis and post-graduation plans. Jori's dream was to become a sports journalist. She'd persuaded her way into internships and at the time, she was sifting through rejection letters while scouring for an opportunity to do the work that she loved. When I told her that I was in the process of planning a fifth trip to Israel, she tells me that she's an Orthodox Jew.

Me: *So you practice Shabbat?*

Her: *Absolutely.*

Me: *Well, how are you going to cover sports and stay true to your religion?*

Her: *I'll make it work.*

And she did. At the time of writing this book, Epstein is an award-winning senior NFL reporter for Yahoo! Sports. And, yes, she practices Shabbat.

Shabbat dates back thousands of years and has its roots in the book of Genesis and Deuteronomy. After the destruction of the Second Temple in 70 CE, rabbis codified the practice through textual interpretations in the Talmud and Mishnah. Over time, various prohibitions and allowances have grown around the practice. It is a day of rest that begins on Friday before sunset and ends after sunset on Saturday.[10]

A year ago, I found myself in a constant state of anxiety. I was traveling every week for my work and noticed an unhealthy relationship that I had with my phone. As soon as my alarm sounded, I would turn it off, and then start scrolling. On some mornings, I'd spend 10 minutes and on other mornings, I might scroll for 30 minutes. During the day, I'd post something on LinkedIn and then spend the next two hours refreshing the app to see how many "likes" or "reposts" I had garnered.

The breaking point came one Friday when I picked up my oldest daughter from school. Although Austin traffic can't be compared to Houston or Los Angeles, it's still bad. In standstill traffic, my daughter starts recounting her day at school and I immediately picked up my phone. As my attention spilled into the phone, I could faintly hear her asking me a question.

Her: *Dad, are you listening to me?*

I wasn't. I could not remember a single episode from her day because Instagram held my attention. I thought of Jori's adherence to her faith while working in a business that operates on a 24-hour news cycle. Just before sunset, I sent a text message to a few people (the ones who might actually need me for important messages) and asked them to relay any 911 messages to my bride, Hilary. I turned off my phone and placed it in my backpack.

I did not turn it on until Sunday night and even then only to set my alarm for Monday. The Friday antsies turned into Saturday bliss. Instead of checking to see if I had added any additional LinkedIn followers, I played football with my kiddos. I thumbed through books. I stared out of my window. I planted tomato seeds. Sure, the first 24 hours was difficult because I had grown dependent on the device. I found myself patting my pockets as if I had lost something. But on Sunday, I felt free. For the past year, I have practiced what I call Cell Shabbat on a weekly basis. What started as a lark has turned into a ritual that my family expects and admires. With just 48 hours of separation from my phone, I enter the new week feeling renewed. And my biggest concern, "What if I miss something important" has failed to materialize. When I check my email, text messages, and LinkedIn account on Sunday night, the world hasn't skipped a beat.

When things aren't working in our lives, we tend to invoke the law of addition. We rush to Amazon to buy a quick fix. Our consumer-centric psyches kick in. But what if the solution lies in taking things away? Small tweaks to the

people, places, and things around us can alter our lives for
the better.

Law 14: Aim for 10 Minutes Instead of 10,000 Hours

Malcolm Gladwell's blockbuster, *Outliers: The Story of
Success*, popularized the idea of the 10,000-hour rule.
Gladwell wrote, "Ten thousand hours is the magic number
of greatness."[11] The central idea is based on research
conducted by the Swedish psychologist Anders Ericcson
and Jacqui Smith. Ericsson was particularly interested in
identifying what accounted for the success achieved by elite
performers. He studied a variety of fields, from music to
sports. His research led him to conclude that people who
engage in deliberate practice achieved high levels of success
within their chosen domain.[12]

What is deliberate practice? In 2008, the journalist
Geoff Colvin latched on to Ericsson's work and published
*Talent Is Overrated: What Really Separates World-Class
Performers from Everybody Else*. I assigned the text as required
reading for most of my classes at the University of
Texas. Colvin writes, "Deliberate practice requires discipline,
focus, and a commitment to continuous improvement."[13]

When Gladwell's book first hit bookshelves, the idea
spread at a frenetic pace. Let's do some quick math. Ten
thousand hours is equivalent to 600,000 minutes, which
works out to roughly 416 days. Obsessing over the large
numbers is enough to cause someone to think, "Well if

I only do 10 minutes then it would take me too long to get to 10,000 hours."

A friend of mine was a realtor in Austin and was considering a career switch. We were talking during the height of the COVID lockdown. Like so many others, he was evaluating every corner of his life and, in particular, he was taking a hard look at his lack of fulfillment in the real estate industry. What did he really want to do with his life? Well, Shawn wanted to be a lawyer. He always jokes, "You threw your law degree away, and I had to nearly kill myself to get one."

His decision to go to law school didn't make sense on paper. He was a top producer in his office, and selling property in Austin during the early 2020s was like playing a game of pickup basketball against a team of toddlers. He would joke, "Heck, half the time I don't even have to physically show the property to anybody. My last nine sales came through Facetime walk-throughs and the buyers made outlandish offers on the spot. All cash."

But selling real estate didn't light Shawn up. Practicing law is what he really wanted to do, but there was just one problem: his age. "If I start law school this fall, I'll be . . ." pausing to do the math, " . . . I'll be 43 when I graduate."

I remained silent and then asked him a simple question "How old would you be in three years if you didn't go to law school?"

"You still there?" I asked.

"Damn, I never thought about it that way, D. F*#k it, I'm doing it."

To be honest, I didn't believe he'd *actually* do it. But before I knew it, he was texting me questions about the LSAT. I still have the text chain.

Shawn: *D, how can I get good at these logic games? They're killin' me, bro.*

Me: *Break this into microwins. Buy this book on Amazon in the next 10 minutes.*

I attached a screenshot of an LSAT study guide. Within three minutes, he sent a screenshot of the Amazon confirmation screen.

Shawn: *Now what?*

Me: *Wait for the damn book.*

Shawn: (Monkey covering his ears emoji)

When the book arrived the next day, he sent a screenshot of the box.

Shawn: *Now what?*

Me: *Start with the introduction and read for 10 minutes.*

Shawn: *Dude. . . I can do more than 10 minutes.*

Me: *I know. Do 10.*

This interaction went on and on for weeks. Before long, Shawn was taking practice tests. Then he signed up for the actual test, and before I knew it, I received this text:

Me: *I got into law school, bro! Moving to Houston in a month!*

Today, Shawn is a practicing attorney in Houston and it all began with buying a book and spending 10 minutes a day studying it.

Let's take that macrowin that you want to achieve. You could scoff at spending 10 minutes a day whittling away at the goal, and never get started. But here's a question: how long will it take if you *don't* spend 10 minutes a day? Don't chuckle. Sit with that thought experiment. How long would it take you if you didn't spend 10 minutes a day? We both know the answer. You'd never arrive at your intended destination. Mastery emerges from the menial. The down and dirty, no-one-can-see-me kind of work.

No crowds are going to erupt after your set of two pushups or 10 minutes of reading. No confetti will fall when you take a 10-minute walk with your child or spend 10 minutes in your garden. But trust me. Keep stacking those 10-minute microwins and watch your life change.

Law 15: Push Through the P-Trap

I enjoy the art of writing. It is a full-body experience.

Hairs standing on the back of the neck . . . tummy-churning . . . fingers trembling ever so slightly as the right words descend from brain to keyboard. When the words are flowing, there isn't a better feeling in the world. When the words aren't flowing, well, it is agony.

Richard Powers is one of my favorite living authors. Because I wanted to meet him in person, I created a Google alert for his name. Every two weeks, I would receive every mention of Powers's name on the World Wide Web. That bimonthly email led me to the Tremont Writers Conference. Powers would be one of the guest lecturers.

The application process was fairly straightforward: a work of fiction, nonfiction, or poetry not to exceed 5,000 words. The work needed to be submitted within 50 days. I was reading the conference's website very early one weekday morning, trying not to make any shrieks that would stir my wife and children. This was my chance to break into the world of fiction and meet my hero.

At my kitchen table I made a commitment: "We're going after this, Daron," I whispered to myself. I thought of my macrowin of becoming a published fiction writer. I opened a new tab in my browser and googled, "How do I write a short story?" and went to work.

As I started brainstorming ideas for my short story, I noticed the recurring hesitation. It's that moment right before fingertips descend on the keyboard. Anyone who has dabbled in the creative arts can identify with that moment of petrification. An idea finds its way into the spine, slides down a shoulder, and tickles the tricep until it reaches a sunken place: the elbow. I like to think of that "dip" as the body's p-trap. It's where creative ideas go to die.

The earliest days of plumbing were plagued with myriad issues, none more tantamount than the need of a barrier between the sewage system and a building's interior. The earliest traps were simple bends in the pipes, but these were not very effective at retaining water and preventing the stinky stuff from invading folks' dinnertime.

The modern p-trap was patented by Alexander Cumming. Cumming's day job was clockmaker, but at night, he tinkered with pipes whose purpose was to catch material that could clog the sewer line or drain.

In that trap lies doubt, overthinking, opinions, shame, fear, baggage. They are formidable barriers and to dislodge them requires deep plunging. In the meantime, just keep typing. And by "typing" I'm not just talking about "writing." Writing is my form of plunging, but your process might look, feel, and smell very different. Keep getting the debris out there before your subconscious has a chance to snatch it back. Your macrowins will breathe in the boldness of your incessant push. For 50 days, I opened the valve to let my creative thoughts flow.

As I read what I wrote, 90% of it lacked any redeeming qualities whatsoever, but I kept finding the 10% that had potential. I kept building. I'd edit. I built some more. I took a quick break. Then I wrote some more. At the same time that I submitted the short story for the writers' conference, I also submitted the article to 12 publications. The conference said yes. The publications said no.

That's what happens in life. Keep plunging to get to yes.

Law 16: Practice Self-Gratitude

Here's some quick trivia: Who is the 2,651st star on the Hollywood Walk of Fame? The answer is Calvin Cordozar Broadus Jr. also known as Snoop Dogg, and on November 19, 2018, he delivered an instant classic in his acceptance speech: "I want to thank me for believing in me, I want to thank me for doing all this hard work. I wanna thank me for having no days off. I wanna thank me for never quitting. I wanna thank me for always being a giver and trying to give more than I receive. I wanna thank me for trying to do more right than wrong. I wanna thank me for being me at all times . . ."[14]

This display of self-gratitude came after he had thanked some of the influential people in his life and although many observers found it offensive, I loved watching every second of it. The term *self-care* has reached hashtag infamy in recent years but I want to make the case for self-gratitude. In fact, I see self-gratitude as an invaluable form of self-care.

We can agree that gratitude is a good thing, and I'm finding the practice is becoming virtually extinct. There is a gas station not too far from my home that is consistently more expensive than its competitors. Nothing on the inside differs from what you would see in a traditional gas station. It has the same snacks, beer, and carbonated drinks that you see everywhere else, but what differentiates this store from its peers is customer service. As soon as the bell above the door rings on a customer's entry, the staff jump into action. "Good morning, how are you? Is there anything that you're looking for in particular?" I've stopped in this gas station during every season of the year, both early in the morning and late at night, and the customer service is always the same.

Although I am a stickler for efficiency, I bypass the credit card scanner at the pump. Much to the chagrin of my children, I go inside just to have real conversations with people who are about to take my money. At the end of every transaction, I hear the same five words, "We really appreciate your business." I choose this gas station because they notice and appreciate me.

Why wait to receive gratitude when we can gift it to ourselves?

Daron, thank you for doing that extra set of planks.
Daron, thank you for choosing the oatmeal over cereal.
Daron, thank you for not turning down that game of
    Connect 4 with your kids.

Think of self-gratitude not as a by-product of an inflated ego. Rather, think of self-gratitude as your future self thanking you for a deposit that you made today. It's a recognition that the best parts of our life require sacrifice. We spend our time, talent, and treasure on a daily basis for others. You are the only person who is required to be in attendance at your death. Instead of waiting for others to recognize the small daily sacrifices that we make, let's thank ourselves.

Law 17: The Microwins System Only Works When You Do

In an ideal world, you inject the Microwins System into your daily regimen. You meticulously plot and execute microwins within the three domains of your work, family, and health. Your wins begin to mount, and over time, you stand atop your work with a deep feeling of achievement, like an Olympic goal medalist.

But life is messy. I can tell you from personal experience the deep work in my life has always been met with resistance.

And when I talk about resistance, I'm not referring to external pressures. I'm talking about the battle that rages on the inside. Those internal voices that reach a fever pitch as soon as we decide to wage war against the status quo. Can you hear them? The toxic tunes can play on repeat for so long that it can become difficult to distinguish their lyrics from white noise. But, the melodies remain.

Perhaps the most common question I get from people is simply this: how do you know when it's time to give up? In spring 2001, I can vividly remember opening that letter-sized envelope from Harvard Law School.

"I am writing to inform you that the Committee has decided to place your application on our waiting list in hopes there will be an opportunity to admit you into the Class of 2004." That's the only sentence that I can remember. Standing in my apartment complex's mail room, I could feel my knees wobble. This was the end. Seventeen years of weaving through the educational rat maze led me to this: the end of my educational existence. Or so I thought. At the precise moment when I read the first sentence of that letter, I was convinced that my professional future was over.

I immediately shut myself off from the world. I didn't go out. I skipped class (why did it matter anymore?). I called in sick to my job. It took me three weeks to recover. Shame slowly subsided into disillusionment and finally crystallized into resolve. For the next three years, I harassed the admissions committee with a letter-writing campaign. I wrote "letters of continued interest." I hunted down University of Texas alumni who had also graduated from Harvard Law School and asked them to write recommendations. And each application cycle, I received the exact same response with one difference—the date at the top.

Why didn't I stop? Honestly, I don't know. I listened to my belly more than my brain. The ending of this saga (finally getting accepted after four admissions cycles) makes this drama sound like a success story. But 20 years removed from that time leaves with me with a greater takeaway: the victory was not in the admission, but the refusal to stop applying.

I can't tell you when it's time to give up on your goals. Three months, three years, three decades? In a world plagued with uncertainty, no decision tree holds the answer to that question. If your macrowin is big enough and your belly loud enough, you'll keep going. Bronnie Ware, a former palliative care provider, spent eight years tending to the needs of people nearing death. She asked them about their regrets. What had they wished they had done more or less of? The most common response was "I wish I'd had the courage to live a life true to myself, not the life others expected of me."[15]

On the first day of teaching each semester, I would show this quote to my students. College classrooms brim with youth. Whenever I would advance toward this particular slide in my PowerPoint, the room would shift.

So, when should you give up? Well, that is a decision that only you can make. I cannot predict what day will be your last. I don't know how many sunrises are left in your lifetime. But what I can tell you is that the days are long.

Life is short. And you are still alive. Never make a long-term decision during a period of short-term despair. Don't give in before taking a breath, silencing your brain, and listening to your belly. You've got this.

Where Do We Go From Here?

You're excited to get going, so let's get this party started.

Craft Your Macrowins

Go back to Chapter 6. There, you'll find the blueprint for sharpening your macrowins for work, family, and health. Typically, I take two weeks in December to dive into this process, but don't let the calendar beat you. It doesn't matter when you start; what matters is that you start.

IT DOESN'T MATTER WHEN YOU START; WHAT MATTERS IS THAT YOU START.

Build Daily Microwins   Remember, perfection is not the goal. We are disciples of consistency. Start small and evaluate your progress. If you're not making progress, go smaller.

This isn't a race or standardized test; this is your life. Treat it with the slowness that you deserve.

Most of the time, I use 4×6 index cards to chart my daily progress, but I've also used Starbucks napkins and sticky notes.

Some days I go 0-for-3 and some days I go 3-for-3. But every single day, I keep going. And that's what you're going to do. You're going to stay the course and if you're looking for extra support, don't forget Law 12.

Recruit Your Roommates Don't read *roommates* too literally. They could be coworkers, family members, or besties. Every Sunday night, we host a "Roberts Family Meeting" in our home and all seven us of share our microwins for the upcoming week.

So, here's your nudge to convince your people to join you. Compare notes. Share what techniques are working. Encourage each other, and make sure you do the following.

Share Your Progress (#Microwins) Someone out there needs a nudge to keep going, and that nudge could come from you. I'll give you an example.

I routinely post my microwins on Instagram. A few years ago, a woman reached out to me on Instagram:

> Thank you so much for posting your microwins! I've got big goals and high hopes. I also have 1 million plates that I'm spinning all the time. Establishing daily microwins was a total paradigm shift that makes

bigger life goal achievement more than hopes for "someday." Microwins reshaped my big goals into daily dragons that I can slay and gave me reason to celebrate small successes along the way.

The Microwin System inspired me to take a leap of faith that I didn't think I had in me. Becoming a small business owner seemed completely out of reach to me until I started processing the dream of being my own boss in daily bite-size achievements. Microwins took something huge and transformed it into a daily challenge that I could wrap my head around and own.

Jamie Sulle, co-owner of The Way Home,
Organizing Solutions

Three years later, Jamie is celebrating the third anniversary of her organizing company with her cofounder and sister, Katie. And it all started when these two women decided to join forces. They agreed to hold each other accountable for small actionable progress toward their goal of entrepreneurship. And today, they are bona fide business owners.

Jamie and Katie are talented people but it's neither their talent nor intelligence that enabled them to accomplish their macrowin. No, it was consistency coupled with a refusal to heed the call of their naysayers.

Remember . . .

You are neither too young nor too old, and it is neither too early nor too late to build the life you deserve. Stay the course, and I'll see you in the deep end.

Oh, wait, one last thing!

Join Us and Get Free Stuff

We are committed to supporting you on this journey. Our team has built a vault of inspirational goodies to keep you headed in the right direction.

Scan the following QR code to download microwins resources and join the movement.

SCAN CODE TO JOIN THE
MICROWINS MOVEMENT

WWW.MICROWINS.CO

Notes

Introduction

1. Think of Black Monday as the inverse of Black Friday. It's the Monday after the last regular season game in the National Football League. Traditionally, it's the day that most head coaches (and by extensions, their assistant coaches) are fired. In recent times, the firing squad has steadily pushed its date of execution earlier in the season.
2. I can hear you judging me. Please take into account that it had been a rough morning. I was fired in the shortest meeting in the history of meetings.
3. Yes, you read that correctly. My head coach had been fired but the assistant coaches were still under contract. So, we showed up to work, pushed some papers around and walked through the hallways to make it look as if we were being productive. All of us understood that as soon as the next head coach was hired, we would be officially axed.
4. In a previous life, I spent three years in law school, which is to say that I read, wrote, and rewrote more words than I care to estimate.
5. Or if you *did* check this book out from the library, then keep a notebook nearby.

Chapter 1

1. Some of you urban readers are wondering, "Why was she talking about a creek?" Well, in rural areas and before the advent of good roads, heavy rains would overrun a lot of the roads that people traveled on. So, a flooded creek could literally divert one's plans.
2. The Plan II website states, "Plan II differs from most honors programs in that its core curriculum is a major. Plan II is a carefully designed core curriculum honors major with very specific multidisciplinary course requirements and strong emphasis on problem-solving, critical and analytical skills, and particularly on writing—including a capstone thesis requirement."
3. Although I'd like to blame the fact that I never followed through with this idea on my wife, I have to admit I never mustered the courage to actually do it.
4. I just made this word up because it sounds better alongside *survival*.
5. I used fictitious names in these excerpts.
6. Maya Angelou interview. Civil rights (May 7, 2019). www.youtube .com/watch?v=90VWA-obyWA.

Chapter 2

1. https://www.merriam-webster.com/dictionary/busyness
2. The names are fictitious but the conversation is real. You're probably thinking, "Daron seems nosey." I like to think of myself as a conscientious observer of humanity. Also, they were talking loudly.
3. At the time of writing, the check engine light might be on permanent display in the dashboard of my car.
4. If you raised your hand, get help.
5. If you can relate, hold a lighter in the air like you just don't care . . . but don't set your blanket on fire.
6. And I'm not even a big fan of dogs. Actually, I like dogs, but I can't stand the way some humans treat their dogs nicer than they treat other humans.
7. Is it just me or does the number of "Giving Tuesdays" balloon each year?

8. I can hear you, "Daron, you've got a system for everything." And yes, you're right. Systems are the antidote to stress.
9. Remember: keep it simple. This isn't your 12th grade English class and you're not Toni Morrison. Follow the playbook.

Chapter 3

1. When I first heard my neighbor say this, my mind immediately went to former Michigan football head coach Jim Harbaugh's locker room battle cry, "Who's got it better than us?" to which the Wolverine players would respond, "Nobody!"
2. Remember those days? There's nothing like having absolutely nothing to lose except for your pride but also being too young to care.
3. I'm a chronic journaler.
4. And, no, I don't have any desire to dip my toe into the cesspool of American politics.
5. Just typing those words (and rereading them) brings a smirk to my face.
6. Or as the young people say, "For the 'gram!"

Chapter 4

1. I am a fan of Jackson's work and my reference relates to the character type that he often plays and not the man who he is.
2. Neff, K. (n.d.). What is self-compassion? Retrieved from https://self-compassion.org/what-is-self-compassion/

Chapter 5

1. Go big or go home. (2022). Grammarist. https://grammarist.com/idiom/go-big-or-go-home/
2. If you met me during this part of my life, I'm sorry. I blame my personality during that time period on the Red Bull.

Chapter 6

1. At least I hope they don't.
2. Collins, J. C., & Porras, J. I. (1994). *Built to last: Successful habits of visionary companies* (HarperBusiness).

Chapter 7

1. If you haven't seen this 1990s classic be sure to check it out.

Chapter 9

1. Christensen, C. (2010, July). How will you measure your life? *Harvard Business Review*. https://hbr.org/2010/07/how-will-you-measure-your-life

Chapter 10

1. Oleribe, O. O., et al. (2018). Health: Redefined. *The Pan African Medical Journal, 30,* 292. https://www.ncbi.nlm.nih.gov/pmc/articles/PMC6320447/#:~:text=The%20word%20%E2%80%9Chealth%E2%80%9D%20is%20derived,definitions%20have%20evolved%20over%20time
2. Fischetti, M., & Christiansen, J. (2021). Our bodies replace billions of cells every day. *Scientific American*. https://www.scientificamerican.com/article/our-bodies-replace-billions-of-cells-every-day/

Chapter 12

1. Williams, S. (2022). Serena Williams says farewell to tennis on her own terms—And in her own words. *Vogue*. https://www.vogue.com/article/serena-williams-retirement-in-her-own-words

2. Tracy, B. (2017). *Eat that frog! 21 great ways to stop procrastinating and get more done in less time* (Berrett-Koehler).

3. Lewis, M. (2012, October). Obama's way. *Vanity Fair.* https://www.vanityfair.com/news/2012/10/michael-lewis-profile-barack-obama

4. Christakis, N. A., & Fowler, J. H. (2007). The spread of obesity in a large social network over 32 years. *New England Journal of Medicine, 357,* 370–379. https://www.nejm.org/doi/full/10.1056/NEJMsa 066082

5. Housman, M., & Minor, D. (2017, May 8). Sitting near a high-performer can make you better at your job. KelloggInsight. https://insight.kellogg.northwestern.edu/article/sitting-near-a-high-performer-can-make-you-better-at-your-job

6. Corsello, J., & Minor, D. (2017, February 14). Want to be more productive? Sit next to someone who is. *Harvard Business Review.* https://hbr.org/2017/02/want-to-be-more-productive-sit-next-to-someone-who-is

7. https://www.youtube.com/watch?v=ioz01-Iah7I

8. Baseball Reference. (n.d.). Hall of Fame batting leaders. Baseball-Reference.com. https://www.baseball-reference.com/awards/hof_batting.shtml

9. Byrne, P. (2009, October 21). The many worlds of Hugh Everett. *Scientific American.* https://www.scientificamerican.com/article/hugh-everett-biography/

10. Posner, M. (n.d.). What is Shabbat?: The Jewish day of rest. https://www.chabad.org/library/article_cdo/aid/633659/jewish/What-Is-Shabbat.htm

11. Gladwell, M. (2008). *Outliers: The story of success* (Little, Brown and Company).

12. Ericsson, K. A., & Schraw, G. (2005). An interview with K. Anders Ericsson. *Educational Psychology Review, 17*(4), 389–412. http://www.jstor.org/stable/23363972

13. Colvin, G. (2010). *Talent is overrated: What really separates world-class performers from everybody else* (Penguin Books).

14. Hollywood Walk of Fame. (n.d.). Snoop Dogg. https://walkoffame.com/snoop-dogg/

15. https://bronnieware.com/blog/regrets-of-the-dying/

About the Author

Top 20 Global Keynote Speaker Daron K. Roberts is a serial reinventor. After graduating from Harvard Law School, he coached in the National Football League and college for seven years. He was fired from the Cleveland Browns in 2013. Daron packed up his family and belongings and moved to Austin, Texas, where he launched the Center for Sports Leadership and Innovation (CSLi) at the University of Texas. After leading that Center and teaching business and leadership courses for eight years, Daron escaped from academia to expand Deep End Ventures, an untraditional leadership dive school where he currently serves as chief dive instructor.

He is the author of *A Kids Book About Empathy* and *Call an Audible*. *A Kids Book About Empathy* was named to Oprah's Favorite Things list and *Call an Audible* was tabbed as a number one new release and best seller by Amazon. *Sports Illustrated* selected the book as one of its "best sports business books" in 2017.

Roberts was honored as LinkedIn's number one top voice in sports and is a graduate of the University of Texas, Harvard Kennedy School, and Harvard Law School.

Daron and his wife, Hilary, chase five children through the streets of Austin, Texas. To learn more about how Deep End Ventures can add value to your team, visit www.coachdkr.com.

Acknowledgments

Writing is hard. Actually, let me rephrase that. Writing is challenging. I like to think of the craft as excruciating euphoria. There's nothing quite like getting an idea or a sentence right. The rub lies in the fact that it takes time, energy, and patience.

This book took the better part of a year to write and the first fruits of my gratitude go to my bride, Hilary. I'm indebted to her for listening to my bursts of frustration and excitement. As with my other two books, she's the first reader whom I can depend on to be both honest and loving with her insights.

I am grateful to The Donut Council—Dylan, Sydney, Jackson, Delaney, and Micah. At some point all of them have asked, "Are you done with that book yet?" Their high-fives and encouraging sticky notes ("Keep going, Daddy!") buoyed me through the highs and lows of the journey.

My parents ensured that I left their home at the age of 18 with a sound belief in my ability to manifest whatever dreams surfaced in my spirit. And my sister was the first writer I ever knew. Her input on this text can be felt throughout the pages of this book.

My chief of staff, Joy Aton-Alejo, helped me to track down sources for some of the most obscure pieces of content. I consume vast amounts of content each day, and Joy helps to keep my litany of bookmarks organized. I am thankful for her willingness to continue to work with me after six long years.

The team at Wiley is a star-studded cast from top to bottom. When Brian Neill first reached out to me about writing a book, we discussed a laundry list of ideas before I arrived at microwins. His early belief in this project set in motion the book you're holding right now. Special thanks also goes to my editor, Tom Dinse. And for the immaculate graphic design work, I tip my hat to the incomparable FaithNiyi.

At the time of writing this book, there are 3,284 people who subscribe to my monthly "Stay In The Deep End" newsletter. Our conversations about personal growth helped me to solidify the principles in this book.

Finally, I am grateful to the hundreds of humans who have used the Microwins System to reach new levels in their life journey. From starting a new business to repairing a broken marriage, their feedback and testimonials forced me to share this practice with the rest of the world. Thank you for being courageous.

Index